THE GODDESS CHANGES

Felicity Wombwell studied textile design at Middlesex Polytechnic and subsequently qualified as a creative arts therapist, working both with individuals and groups. She is a consultant at the Serpent Institute in London, and also works in financial administration for two environmental charities. She has a very strong commitment to deep ecology and environmental concerns, especially in the community.

Felicity has studied and worked with the Goddess in the Grecian, alchemical, Celtic, Dianic and women's mystery traditions of magic and the mysteries. She is a Priestess of both the women's mysteries and in the Fellowship of Isis. She lectures and leads workshops on the Goddess throughout the country.

D0452234

THE GODDESS CHANGES

A personal Guide to Working with the Goddess

BY FELICITY WOMBWELL

Illustrations by Mocha and Paul Brady

Mandala

An Imprint of HarperCollins*Publishers*

Mandala
An imprint of HarperCollins*Publishers*
77–85 Fulham Palace Road,
Hammersmith, London W6 8JB

Published by Mandala 1991

1   3   5   7   9   10   8   6   4   2

A CIP catalogue record for this book is available from the British
Library

ISBN 1-85274-111-2

Printed in Great Britain by
Woolnough Bookbinding Ltd.,
Irthlingborough, Northamptonshire

Typeset by Burns & Smith Ltd., Derby.

*In memory of
John-Kennedy
and
Lucy*

ACKNOWLEDGEMENTS

Acknowledgements for this book go to all those who helped me while I was writing.

Special thanks to:

Paul Brady who did some of the illustrations and whose constant help and encouragement kept me going even when I wanted to run and hide.

John and Caitlín Matthews who have helped me through all the stages of the work both practically and with their constant support and encouragement.

Penny who was the encouraging Guardian of the Threshold.

Mocha who understood the illustrations without me really having to explain.

Peter who helped both with the reading and with ideas.

Ruth who read the manuscript with only a moment's notice.

Michael for the long conversations of encouragement.

To my fellow members of the magical groups that I am part of.

To those that have come to me for help. Helping them has sorted out my own ideas.

To Marija Gimbutas whose pictures inspired a thousand images.

To all the weavers and spinners of the past whose work I have admired in galleries and museums and who have encouraged my belief in the work.

To Mary Daly for her work on the Spinner. This was where I originally got the idea for the work.

To Jack for his interpretations of the progress of the work.

To all at the Ecology Centre who have been so understanding while I was writing.

To Olivia Robertson who showed me the way to find the Voice of the Goddess in her oracle.

And to all those that have helped me be a Priestess of the Goddess.

The mystery of giving birth is basically associated with the ideas of spinning and weaving and complicated feminine activities consisting in bringing together natural elements in a certain order.

M.L. Von Franz, *The Feminine in Fairytales*

The warp was woven at noon
The woof in the house of dawn
The rest in the hall of the sun

Wrought on the loom
Danced on the threads
Golden grown woven for the moon
Shimmering veil for the little sun.

E. Neumann *Eastonian Song*

To weave is not merely to predestine, and to join together differing realities but also to create, to make something of one's own substance as the spider does in spinning the web.

Women's wisdom lies only in the spindle.

Talmud (quoted in the Guardian 25.7.90 'When Faith and Feminism Clash')

The Spinster is a witch she is denied because she is free and therefore feared.

Mary Daly *Gyn/Ecology*

In the beginning was not the word.
In the beginning is the hearing
Spinsters spin deeper into the listening
deep
We can all spin what we hear.

Mary Daly *Gyn/Ecology*

To be created by Changing Woman is to start from the sacred feminine the place of communion and relationship and substantial fullness.

Sheila Moon *Changing Woman and Her Sisters*

CONTENTS

INTRODUCTION TO THE MYSTERIES OF THE CHANGING OR WEAVING GODDESS

This book is about the Weaving Goddess or Changing Woman. She is the changing aspects in women. These aspects are represented by the Fates of Greek mythology, and by the spider. They are represented in the three worlds by the spider in the lower world, Changing Woman in the middle world, and the Weaving Goddess in the upper world. There is also the hidden or veiled aspect of the Goddess, which is the part that is resting.

These worlds can also be described as the world of the dark or the spider, the twilight or the changing world, the realm of Changing Woman and the light golden world, the place of the Weaving Goddess. Within each of these worlds the Goddess or the woman has four aspects, which are best represented by the spinner, the weaver, the cutter and the wild woman.

It is a three-layered system, and within each layer are four aspects. So altogether there are 12 different figures. In the first chapter 1 have shown these aspects as represented by some well known Goddesses. Within this are some of the oldest aspects of the Goddess, which are also some of the most hidden.

The book is very personal and relies on the meditations or journeys that I have taken myself. For the most part they are my own ideas, and are not based on historical fact. I have tried to show in the text where I have used others' ideas to stimulate my imagination and where these imaginary journeys have taken me. Therefore not everyone may agree with all that I say. The book is written with the hope of stimulating others' individual research, especially into the self and its place in the world.

As an artist I have been very stimulated by visual images, so much of the book describes my visions. The book is trying to show what happened to me over the last ten years, in which I have been involved in magical groups looking at the Goddess. It is not so much about the Goddess herself as about how I have seen her, how she has helped me in my life, and what has happened as I have followed her path.

The book is a subjective account of the Goddess, but the References at the back contain a list of books on the Goddess that I have found useful. The process of writing this book has taken me through the stages of the Changes of the Goddess in much the same way as I have outlined in the book. The events that I have chosen to remember are also very subjective. I have used the best visions and examples that I could find rather that some of the more ordinary ones. In places I have also tried to show some of the things that can go wrong and some of the disagreements that I have had over the years, but I have left these to a minimum in the hope of showing the positive side while remembering that things do not always go well.

I started my journey to the Goddess and these worlds by reading a book called *The Spiral Dance* by Starhawk.[1] I recall reading it in bed in one day. It said to me what I had always known but somehow had not been able to put into words. I was home. I was on the bridge. I had taken the first steps to find what I had been searching for for many years. This was a way of explaining the energies that I felt moving within myself and within nature.

After reading the book I came into contact with people who had the same ideas as Starhawk. My first introduction to the Goddess came through the Matriarchy group[2] then based at the Woman's Place in London. Through this group I was introduced to books about the history of the Goddess, her images and symbols. Through this study I began to see the images of the Goddess everywhere. I began to understand a language of the spirit and how subtle it is, and also how this language is and was transferred into symbol and story.

The understanding that I received at that time has now been changed by the experiences that I have had since. In order to understand what I experienced and learnt, I have now developed a system to piece all these aspects together. There were several reasons for this, the main one being the wish to explain my ideas and thoughts to others in a simple manner that also contained the complexity of what I was trying to express.

The different worlds are the levels of non-ordinary reality. They exist within and without this ordinary world. When we are in ordinary reality these other worlds do not exist; they are only present when we choose to move to non-ordinary reality. This is the easiest way of describing these worlds, as they are part of our imaginations. Here we have to make a jump, as it is necessary to understand that we do not always control our imaginations and that there is a force outside outselves that we can contact at these times. In ordinary reality we have an imagination, but non-ordinary reality is connected to the whole universe, and we can contact the spirits of the universe to ask for help and wisdom. Unfortunately it is only with personal experience that some of these things can be found to be true.

The four principal Goddesses of these worlds and the journey through the elements of the Goddess are all part of these other worlds. What follows in the next four chapters is the four main changes of the Goddess as I see them when the Goddess appears in my meditations and visions.

RAINBOW GODDESS

I start with the image of Rainbow Goddess. I see her as a shining egg filled with all the colours of the rainbow. She is young, happy and carefree, spinning and spiralling across the vortex of space. She is hunting and searching like a child for new things to discover and consume in answer to an internal prayer that the universe is constantly creating and changing, and she wants to discover what its latest creations have been.

She is the first step towards a consciousness which contains the Goddess as a spiritual principle in our lives. When we contact this aspect we try and find the Goddess as she has been to others and as she has been represented by others, and the places that were once sacred to her.

My first interest in the Goddess came through pictorial representations of her, especially in textiles and other craft works. It also came through the Jungian archetypes.

My journey to the Goddess started when I joined a group of women who were exploring the Goddess in their lives and in history. This group was divided into various sub-groups, and the ones that I immediately felt an affinity with were the ritual group and the art group. Shortly afterwards a Dianic group also started. Together all these groups helped me find my own way to the Goddess. It started by my seeing for the first time her symbols and images in a way that affirmed my existence as a woman, and that made me feel I was real and three-dimensional. Her symbols and images gave me a sense that there was a meaning and a strength in being a woman. Previously I had never been able to answer the question of why I was here on this planet, why there

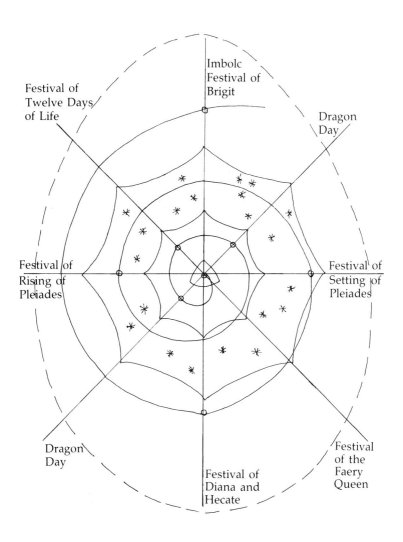

Figure 1 *The festivals of the Goddess*

were both women and men, and why life was the way it was. These are questions that have always fascinated me, and my life seems to be a quest to find a substantial answer to these questions. Previously I had found no philosophy that came anywhere near answering them.

My first involvement with the Goddess answered these questions, because they made the feminine and the masculine sacred through veneration of their forms. There were both good and bad aspects. The Goddess and the pagan Gods come in all shapes and sizes, literally and metaphorically. The symbols of the Goddess are universal and are not just subject to one invading religion. The same is true of the myths and legends associated with her.

Having experienced the Goddess in the Dianic craft, I became very interested in the idea of festivals to the Goddess which were dedicated to the feminine (see Figure 1). For me the eight principal festivals of the year were very much about the cycle of the Goddess and the God (see Figure 2). As I did my research into these festivals, I became convinced that there were festivals to the Goddess in her own right, and that these were what should be celebrated in a woman's group as they seemed to belong to women's cultural heritage. At first I could find very little evidence to show that these existed, but women's history can be found hidden in the prison of old manuscripts. Small clues came to the surface. With these I began to develop my own ideas about how and when women's festivals were celebrated. It started with taking the more easily accessible festivals of the Eleusian Mysteries — the Autumn Equinox, the festival of Diana and Hecate (13 August), and Imbolc (1 February) — then adding to these.

The first discovery that I made was what I called Dragon Day. This is a dual festival celebrated at the time of Equinox and is about the dragon power of the earth rising and falling with the seasons. The energy of the earth visibly rises at this time as the plants start to grow, and falls at the time of the Autumn equinox. Dragons are also sacred to the feminine and the energies of the earth.

Another discovery was the rising and setting of the Pleiades, which occurs at the beginning of May and of November. The Pleiades are also called the Seven Sisters, so I thought that this was a good time to celebrate a women's festival, especially in a group of women. These stars are related to many of the stone circles and to the sailing seasons of old. They were the stars that guided ships. They follow the path of the sun through the

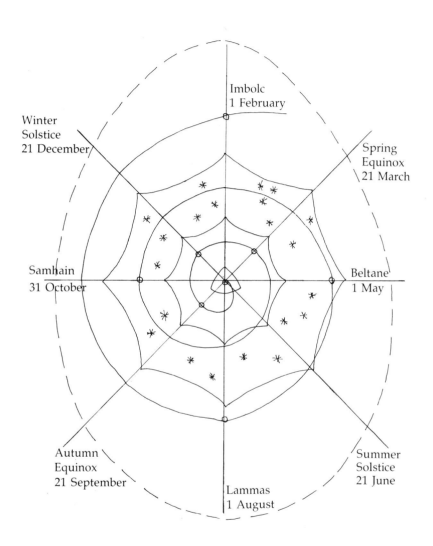

Figure 2 *The seasonal festivals of the year*

heavens and give rise to the sun shining at midnight. In the northern hemisphere they are not visible between May and October. As they are a cluster of seven stars, they are said to relate to the seven sacred planets and to the seven energy centres of the body. Maia is the mother of the Pleiades, the veiled one hidden in the summer months. She is the Goddess of the veil covering the hidden mysteries of the Goddess.

From research into the Celtic mysteries came the festival of the twelve days of Christmas — or the twelve days after the sun is born at the dark of the year. These days are traditionally linked with the giving of gifts, and in ancient times they were the gifts of the mother to her children to show that they had grown up. This festival is connected to Arianrhod and the spinning castle, symbolizing the movement of time about the axis of life. The twelve days represent twelve years. In Celtic times children were considered to be adult at the age of twelve. The mother would then give her children adult names, and also the tools of their trade. We used this idea very successfully in one group which was just starting up, and on this day gave the group its new magical tools. On the Solstice we gave the group its name. This festival has much potential for revival, and could have many uses.

February has the festival of Brigit, the Goddess of birth. Although Brigit has been turned into a saint, I think that she has much to offer women, and her mysteries are very strong in the British Isles — in fact the British Isles are named after her. She is celebrated as the midwife, the virgin and the bride. Her connection to these mysteries is the rush cross that is used to represent her. This cross has four arms which could represent the four elements and the four seasons. She is the Woman of the sacred flame which burnt eternally in Kildare, Ireland. She is also associated with the hearth, which was a place of great sacredness to earlier peoples. She is the Goddess of the Augury or weather forecasting, and also associated with the ewes' milk and the spring lambing. This event is very important to the Weaving Goddess, as it is from the sheep that the wool comes for spinning.

These are some of the mysteries that I discovered about the Rainbow Woman — the woman who goes out and searches and discovers. She is the maiden or the spinning aspect of the Goddess. She is like the rainbow around the moon. She is the going out rather than the going in.

WARRIOR WOMAN

Warrior Woman is the weaving aspect of the Goddess of Change. She is the aspect that puts together all the pieces that have been found in the voyage of discovery of Rainbow Woman. In the process of weaving, the threads that make up the warp represent the part that we have already discovered. They are our history of the Goddess, our lives so far and our dreams. We then put onto this the weft threads, which are the pattern or picture of our lives. The threads that we have spun are dyed to colours of our choice, and we start to make pictures. Some come from what we need to work with, others from what we would like to happen in our lives. As we work on the images, the picture forms and new aspects are added to the whole.

The picture that we form for Warrior Woman is at first the image of someone going out to fight, but the trickster side of her means that we are often fighting ourselves in order to become awake and alive. As the tapestry grows, so we become more creative and more conscious of the choices that we can make in our lives. The warrior aspect creates the picture of the path that we wish to follow. It helps us make sense of the pattern that we are weaving in our lives.

The trickster side of Warrior Woman is very important, as this is the part that tricks us in action, to start the process of change. She is the woman in her twenties or early thirties who has some experience of life and is now trying to understand what is happening. She has seen life and is beginning to have views on how society and her life should progress. At this age we often get involved in political activity. We also start to look for our own path with the Goddess and the work that we are called to do. We start to find ourselves as Priestesses of the Goddess. We also start to look for others who are also Priestesses so that we can gain support and help with our work.

The Warrior Woman is the warrior for the cause of the Goddess. She can fight for the rights of women, the re-establishment of the rights of the Goddess in society and the ways of the Goddess, so that life can become sacred again. I believe we have to find the Goddess or higher parts of ourselves so that we can find our true self. All these are ways of the Warrior Goddess. All these are part of the tapestry that we weave in our lives, making the picture clearer so that we may all understand it.

DANCING WOMAN

The Dancing Woman is the cutting aspect of the Weaving Goddess. She is like the queens of old. The cutter is the giver of divine justice. She is the one who bakes the cakes of the Goddess, who dyes the cloth and makes the wine — the sacred spirit. The Dancing Woman is the alchemical Goddess in that she consciously makes changes in her life. I found this aspect of the Goddess in my meditation on Astraea. Astraea is the Goddess of the Stars and was the last Goddess to leave the earth. According to legend she left during the Iron Age. She is pictured with the sword and scales of Justice and the sheaf of wheat of the virgin. Within the Fellowship of Isis I am a Priestess of Astraea. For me she is the way forward in my work. I feel that this is the age of the stars and space, and it is space magic that is the way forward for magic.

THE WILD WOMAN

The fourth aspect of the Goddess is the wild woman of the forest or the desert. She is the woman who lives alone and is in contact with all the forces of nature. The wild woman is the woman of creation and power, woman unto herself. She has found both inner and outer freedom, and can love as she chooses. This is the hidden or the veiled aspect of the Goddess. She is behind the veil of nature, so in constant contact with its vital energy. She is both at rest and creative. Hers is the realm of nature and the environment. She is the woman to invoke when we work for the healing of the planet.

Often we find that there is one part of the thread that we wish to align ourselves to more than another. There are numerous paths to the Goddess mysteries, and they are individual to each of us. Most people associate the worship of the Goddess with Wicca or Witchcraft. This is one of many paths to the Goddess.

In modern Witchcraft the female aspect of the Goddess is worshipped as divine as well as the male. She becomes the head of the Group as represented through the Priestess. The Wiccan path follows the Goddess as she changes through the seasons and as her relationship to the God changes. Her power as the Moon is worshipped and also as the mother of the earth. Unfortunately Witchcraft has had a very bad press because it has been confused with Satanism. I have never come across any person who calls themselves a Witch and worships Satan. Worshippers of Satan usually call themselves Satanists, and they do not follow the changing cycle of the seasons.

Many women are attracted to Witchcraft because it venerates the feminine. The Wiccan way of following the seasons and the cycles of the moon is a very beautiful way of following the Goddess. It celebrates the seasons and the passing of time, and gives markers to our fast life. We have the chance to stop and think about the last six weeks of our lives. What have we done, what have we achieved, and how do we want to change the way things are going at present? Has anything changed since the last time that the group met?

Some women would rather celebrate this change of seasons with women only rather than in mixed groups. This form can be called the Dianic path, though in America there are mixed Dianic groups. Diana is the Goddess of the Moon and the virgin huntress of the forest. Her mysteries were written down by Charles Layland in the late 1800s.[3] The Dianic tradition that I have experience of is the woman-only tradition. In this the cycles of time and the Goddess were celebrated from a woman's point of view. They were about how a woman experiences the change of the seasons and her place within these changes. It was also about finding oneself as a woman within this society, and how this can have a sacred, life-enhancing aspect.

I think that there is a difference between celebrating the festivals in a woman only group and in a mixed group. There is a difference of emphasis and there is also a very different feel. At first this felt very strange to me as I was not used to being in groups of women only and had worked in an all-male preserve. As the group went on I found it very supportive but also very difficult as the way I led my life was very different from some of the other women.

I feel that the Dianic craft is about discovering these differences and how to relate to them. The Dianic group is a celebration of the life changes of woman. It is also about finding our connection to the earth. Dianic mysteries are about the cycles of the moon. These are celebrated at the esbats (the full and new moon), very often in the open. The cycles of the moon are related to the menstrual cycle and are often celebrated in the form of the ovulating and menstruating Goddess. In groups, because of time constraints, we celebrated either the new or the full moon.

These celebrations were very much a celebration of ourselves as women and an enjoyment of what we as women were. These ceremonies came very much from the mood of the group on that particular day, and involved us celebrating what we felt was appropriate to that time. We started by agreeing a particular format and the work that we would like to do. The work was varied but connected to the time of year and what we felt needed to be celebrated. Sometimes we would do a healing, sometimes a working so that changes could happen in individuals' lives. Our rituals were worked out together from the collective experience.

The ritual would begin with some sort of circle opening, usually walking around one three times, or the drawing of a formal circle, or both. Individual women would then do a invocation to the Goddess of the quarters or the primary elements and perhaps a joint invocation to the Great Goddess would be performed. The work would then continue. Sometimes this would be a path working to meet the Great Goddess, sometimes a healing for the earth, the trees, women or animals. There would also be a mention that the moon was changing phase again, and that we were all part of this continuous motion of the heavens. At times the form of the ritual would be chosen by the astrological sign that the moon was in and how we related to that sign. After the work we would have a feast and discussions, which usually focused around the Goddess.

It is the celebratory nature of these meetings that made them feel so good — the feelings of women celebrating together. They are very much about the celebration of friendship that can occur when strong feelings are shared by women together. Very often it is the reason why we decide to keep coming to these celebrations.

For me the celebrations that happened outside in the open air were the most enjoyable and the strongest, probably because our contact with nature and the earth is felt more strongly at these times. Being in a forest or among trees at the full moon is a very magical experience. If the energy of the women involved connects to this magic, then a profound inner experience can happen. The energy of the group can also be connected to the trees. The connection of the energy of the land to the people working in the group is enough for a celebration. But it seems that because we who live in cities never need to touch the earth in our lives, the experience is that much stronger when we do. The celebration of the joining of these sorts of energies is usually expressed by singing and dancing within the circle that we have created. This idea is strongly expressed in the song 'Dancing in the Full Moon Light' and in other chants used at Greenham Common.

Celebrations of this sort are often the only chance we as women have of expressing ourselves in a creative manner. Work and the way we live our lives often leave no time for celebration in a sacred manner. Dance, art, singing and music-making were once sacred activities that everyone participated in. By finding these arts again we have discovered how to make our lives more meaningful and fulfilled.

Ritual to the Full Moon

Find a place that you want to celebrate in. This can be the garden, if you are not over-looked, or a room. Start by finding the objects that you need. Candles are good as these give a different atmosphere than usual. Incense is also good for atmosphere and stimulating the senses. Smell is a sense that is very underused these days. Objects that represent your feelings towards the full moon are good to have around.

If you have no ideas, try sitting outside and looking at the full moon, and see what comes. If you want to get in touch with Diana, you can look in the local history section of your library and find where shrines to Diana have been found locally. She was a very popular Goddess in the Roman era and there are many places that were once shrines to her worship. Many of these no longer exist in their original form, but often the local history will give impressions of how the area looked in the last century. It is only in recent times that places have changed so dramatically. This can help towards finding a way that you would like to celebrate the full moon, alone or as part of a group.

Now use your intuition to guide you as to what to do. The first time that you do a ritual you might feel a bit silly talking to no one. This soon passes. The energy and feelings of the Goddess will then enter your body and you will feel a great rush of energy. The feelings that you receive from this are the magic that you are looking for.

I feel that I am now a Priestess of the Goddess and that this is what I was striving for, although I did not know it at the time. For the last eight years I have been a member of a Women's Magical Group. This has had some constant members but mainly consisted of different people as the group changed and progressed. This has reflected the constantly changing nature of the mysteries and how they affected those that were part of the groups. The group had to change as our understanding of the Goddess changed and we experienced her more fully. At first I started with just experiencing the mysteries of the Goddess and women, and how these could be made manifest in our lives, and how we could learn from her myths and legends. This was mainly an intellectual quest until the legends began to start working in my life.

I then found that I wanted more and more to worship the true spirit of the Goddess as expressed in my interpretation of her myths and legends and that I was not interested in doing other interpretations of her at this stage. What I did not realize was that I was trying to find her from myself and that to do this I had to understand how she manifested in my life. At first I tried to find her through the cycle of the seasons and through fitting rituals to her festivals, later in relating the Goddess to the cycles of the moon. At this time there was no indication in my work for me to dedicate myself in a particular Goddess or to a particular path. Even at that time I was working towards a rather independent form of magic.

I started in a group that explored what the mysteries were and how they manifested in a feminine form. I then moved to study the Celtic path. With some friends we formed a group to study these mysteries, and it was through this group that I started to find the mysteries that I truly related to personally.

For me the mysteries at first were the study of the mystical in life and myself, and were not related to any particular Goddess or path. They were about finding the Goddess within, and it was like walking through a labyrinth to discover what would be inside. The path of the Goddess is long and labyrinthine and can take you to unexpected and unexplored parts of yourself and the universe.

The Goddess is within us all as a guide to answer the problems of life and show us how we can overcome them. She is the higher part of ourselves that we can easily ignore and not acknowledge in ourselves. We all have within us the ability to answer all our questions, if only we have the patience and take time.

The Goddess path was the first of the mystery religions that I came across. This was very important for me as it started to answer the questions that I could not as yet answer for myself. I continued to follow it through thick and thin, because it was for me a way to find the source of my power and identity. My quest for the Goddess was my quest for myself.

The spinner can be angry and spin faster and faster and faster as the anger rises, and then slower as the anger is released. As the emotions intensify, the colours of the rainbow become stronger and then fade.

The weaver weaves faster and faster, and the cloth form at speed as the feelings are connected; then they relax when the fight is over.

The dancer dances the dance of the changing feelings. This becomes the dance of the universe.

The wild woman becomes a monster as the feelings intensify, and then changes into the void when she has released the feelings. It is only when we try to hold these feelings that things start to go wrong. She taught me that it was all right to feel and be a feeling person, and this was how I began to find out who I was and what there was to life.

This is the cycle of the Weaving Goddess, the Changing Woman within ourselves. The book contains my thoughts and ideas about working with the Goddess. It also has some practical rituals, and a reference section with further reading on each subject and contact addresses of groups who work in a similar way.

The book is a personal quest and I hope that it will stimulate others to go on their own quest.

$$=== 1 ===$$

THE SPIRAL OF THE SEASONS

The spiral tendency within each one of us is the longing for and growth towards wholeness.[1]

The old calendar was divided up into periods of roughly six weeks. At the end of each period there was a festival to mark the change of season. Each festival has a Weaving Goddess or a woman of change associated with that time of year (Figure 3). These Goddesses act as an introduction to the idea of a Weaving Goddess and show how her aspects have been incorporated into the mythology of other Goddesses. Like Isis the Changes of the Goddess have a thousand names. The cycle of change around the year can be seen as having a dark and a light side. Each light festival has a corresponding dark festival.

THE RAINBOW

The Spring Equinox is on 21 March, when day and night are of equal length, when the sun shines and there is often a lot of rain. It is also the time of the dawn and early morning.

I have always been very attracted to the idea of the rainbow as the bridge to other worlds. Where I lived as a child we were surrounded by a lot of water. The watery realms move and flow with ease, and are not as rigid as the earthy realm. The world of fishes is one of movement and change as they move from one watery landscape to another. In this realm live the spirits of the water that look rather like water weeds. The spirits are the motivations for love and the flow of life in the world. They can bring peace, but also raise up the storms of our emotional lives. As the waters pass us by as we watch, we can either go in and

27

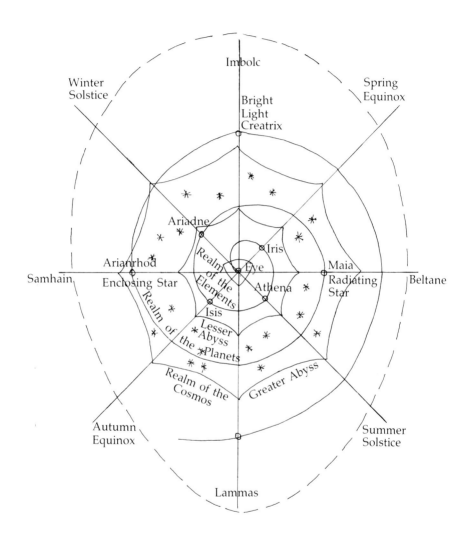

Figure 3 *Weaving Goddesses and women of change associated with festivals*

join them, or sit and watch from the shore, or stand half in and half out and be at peace with them. The realm of the waters is very supportive and reconnects us with the fluidity of life. It is where life started, so it is like going back to the very beginning. It is helpful to meditate on water when new beginnings are in order.

LADY IRIS

In Alchemy Iris is called 'Juno's messenger, and is the harbinger of death to women as mercury is to man. To release the souls of women in alchemy means to sublime the volatile parts of the residue after the *nigredo*, thus producing the rainbow colouring which is called the peacock's tail.'[3] It seems strange to think of the rainbow Goddess as the bringer of death, yet to start the path to the Goddess is very much about death. There is a little death that we have to go through before we can follow her path: to give up our old life before we can carry on with our new-found interest.

I had to make several changes to my life so that I could continue walking this road, including changing my job, becoming more creative and part of a society that was very foreign to me. I changed my relationship to one with more understanding of what I was doing and interested in. Being on this path is not easy, and being involved in magic does not mean that things come easier. If anything, life becomes more difficult as you meet more and more that needs to be changed or healed. It is like opening the flood-gates and everything seems to come out. However, it becomes easier to cope with all the changes as time goes on. My identification with Iris is very much to do with the death aspect of myself. On this path I have found the destructive parts of my character and how I can very easily kill the ideas of others and their life spirit by not really being in contact with my own.

For a very long while I nurtured the spark of creativity in myself, but never really allowed it to grow into a tree. It remained a plant that often died through lack of water. The image of a tree is very central to my being as it is a symbol of the self that I never saw before. In many ways I still don't believe that all I have gone through contains the basis of the tree, but this is because without realizing I have built the tree of my unknowing. This is turning out to be stronger and larger than I thought, and recently I have not been able to see the wood for the tree, or the tree for the branches. I have not burnt the residue to see that in it is the peacock tail. I have not valued my ideas enough.

I have also found that I am the bringer of death to others in that by being with them I have somehow started the process of change in others, and they have had to let go of things that they cherished in order that other changes could happen. I had never before given this task any importance until I was present at the death of a friend and realized how important what I represented to the friend was, that I can enable change in others and that if I am important for others I can be so for myself.

As the spiral crosses the cross of the year, the next meeting point is the time of the Summer Solstice, which is the high point of summer. Here we move from the aspect of the Maiden Spinner to that of the Warrior Weaver.

ATHENA

I was very struck by the image in C. Downings book[3] of Athena presenting to her altar the cloak/shawl that she had made during the previous nine months. I remember a friend of mine presenting her book to the altar of the Goddess and how it seemed so important to present one's own creativity to the Goddess. It is a way of affirming one's own work and acknowledging what has been done by the higher self. It is easy to do, yet difficult to make time for this sort of activity.

Athena is the goddess of household activities: the tasks that we do all the time but that are forgotten and not acknowledged by ourselves or others. So many of women's sacred activities are performed in the house and are therefore not as valued as those that are done outside the home. Athena represents the fighting spirit that we as women need in order to get these activities acknowledged as important and creative. It is often the space and quiet that the home represents that allows us to find these creative sparks to take out and light the world and to weave for the good of others or to earn our living.

Athena wove her own dress. This represents the way that we would like others to see us. Athena carries the shield or the mask with the Medusa's face on it. She is the Goddess of creativity but also has a dark side from which her creativity comes. It is like the compost of the earth or the *prima materia* that is within ourselves, or the darkness from which the light grows. Athena wears both for others to see. She acknowledges the sources from which her inspiration comes and how it is present in her life. I wear my

Medusa mask and very rarely take it off, as this is the part of myself that I identify with most. I am more in touch with my source than with what I have produced from this source. I am also fighting for the acceptance of this force within society, as I feel we spend too much time looking at the light and very little time acknowledging the source of this power in the dark.

This force is feminine in nature. Both the earth and the feminine have become devalued as inspiration for how we can live our lives. For example, the menstrual mysteries have become devalued in our lives, and can no longer be mentioned in public. It is for these reasons that I wear the Medusa mask and for women's sacred parts in general which have become diseased through lack of acknowledgement and no longer the sacred centres of our bodies that they should be.

Dolore Ashcroft-Nowicke has inspired me greatly in this area with her work on the Sacred Chakra and the reconsecrations of the Womb ritual in *The First Steps in Ritual*[4]. I have adapted this ritual and also performed it for other women. I found it a profound experience for myself, and have since seen my womb as the Grail of my life and the inspiration of my work, which can now come from the sacred centre of my body. Doing it for others is a very emotional experience, and the freeing that some women have obtained from the experience cannot be expressed in words.

Since being a candidate in this ritual I have been much more in contact with my own creativity and how important it is in my life at this time. I have always felt that to find one's own creativity was very important and have been doing workshops on this theme for a number of years. For a long time I concentrated on the finding of the spark, but now I am beginning to realize that it also needs to be woven into the dress of our being so that we may form it into something solid and lasting that we can present at our altar to the goddess.

Athena is very much to do with group creative activity, and this is what my workshops are about. If you can show your creativity to others — that you have made this unique piece of work — then this cannot be denied by the self. In the group rituals we have done for the reconsecration of the womb we have witnesses to the renewed sacredness of the body which has now been fully restored. This gives recognition to the newly forming self and to the part of ourselves that wants to be healed. We become the warriors of this cause in ourselves because it is what we need.

It is also what the earth needs, and we do it for her too. She is

31

being raped by society for her treasures at the present moment, and we are using them without realizing that the regenerative process has a limited life. Women also die early if they have too many children. As women we must join together and fight to save the earth and at the same time make her sacred and renewed once more.

Athena holds the bag which contains the sacred vowels of the alphabet. These are the sacred sounds of the universe, which made the universe first turn. It is these sounds that we have to find again for ourselves. They are the sounds of the self which we often lose in our childhoods. They are the sounds of our souls. The next phase of the spiral is the Autumn Equinox, the time of the light going into the darkness. On the inner spiral this is the time of water and of the Sovereign Cutter. The Weaving Goddess who best represents this aspect is Isis.

ISIS

Isis is the supreme deity of the Egyptian Pantheon. As Witt says:

> Isis is the one divinity to whose higher authority Fate (Heimarmene) has at once to bow. Lucius pays homage to his August mother because she can unravel the web of destiny, so twined and twisted together that no other hands than hers know the secret of disentanglement, can tame the storms of fortune, and can check the harmful ways of the stars.[5]

This is the aspect of sovereignty. Isis is the queen of all and the mother of all. It is through finding our own sovereignty that we find the confidence to heal others. Isis is the great healer, which is why the Fates bow to her. It is her girdle of healing that heals all those who wear it. This girdle is the girdle of the stars, which contain the healing totems that can change the harmful ways of the stars. In her aspect of sovereignty we find we are the rulers of our own destinies and can choose how we want to live our lives, what we want to happen, and how we want this to manifest. We become the rulers in our own temples, which are our bodies and the realm in which we live. This includes our relationships, our work and our friendships.

Here we must work in complete consciousness and make a choice that is right for us. This choice can be painful because it might be seen as preferring one thing above another, but this is not the real choice. The real choice is to do what is right for ourselves what ever the cost to others, as otherwise others are not free to make the correct choices for themselves.

I find these decisions the hardest of all to make as I constantly put others before myself and don't value my own needs, and also worry about what others will think. It took me a long time to learn that if you tell others what you need they often respond very positively, and you can then negotiate about how your needs can fit in with others' needs.

Sovereignty also means independence so that you are able to

Figure 4 *The knots of Isis*

do as you want. It is being free of others' projections so that you know that what you want is really what you want and not what others want you to have. Independence is essential for the work of healing, so that you can clearly see what the cause of the problem is, without being influenced by any preconceived feelings or thoughts. It is also about being able to just listen rather than giving advice so that the person may find for themselves the healing part of themselves. Advice and help are not always necessary. We have to learn to stay in contact with our bodies and centred so that we can truly feel the emotion body of our being.

The knot of Isis represents the knot that ties us to our true being. It ties all the levels together, and this is plaited together to form a fourth that is tied to keep all in the centre (Figure 4). The knot is then tied over the heart of the sacred centre of the person. It also keeps the robe of Athena in place. The knot makes the Ankh or the symbol of life. Isis brings things to life in all her aspects. She brought Osiris back from the dead as well as Horus. She is also the representative of the living earth, and it is under her aegis that the Nile floods and brings life to the earth. She works with the people on the land bringing to life plants like a midwife.

Her symbol is also the throne. She sits on it in her sovereign aspect as the overseer and judge of all things. The throne represents the earth and the Goddess of the land. On the throne sits the king, and by sitting here he shows his union with the sacred nature of all things. It is from here that the sovereign gives judgement. This is the judgement of wisdom and the judgement of the relationship with nature. If you give judgement from this place you give the truth of the world and how things fit together. By sitting here you prevent the judgement being subjective. The throne is like sitting in the lap of the Goddess, and she gives the oracle to which you can add the facts to aid the understanding of the judgement.

It is important to find the position of the throne in a room and make it into your sacred centre. As within so without. When I see clients I sit in a seat beside the hearth, which is the traditional seat of the Goddess within the house. I did not do this consciously, but by moving around the room until I found the place that was right for me to sit in. This is like the knot of my work and the place from which I can be centred. It is from here that one can reach up to the crown of the stars and down into the depths of the earth. Thus one is connected to all the realms and with the body of the self.

Isis and her mythology are very like the individuation process in Jungian psychology. She originated in Neith the virginal Creatrix who gives birth to the self. Then she became the daughter of the Earth, then the wife of Osiris, then his saviour, and finally the woman enough unto herself and the principal deity of the ancient world. Her relationship to the God is very important as it represents the relationship to her animus of her inner self.

Isis is the goddess who shows us the ways to access this material, because in the mythology she goes through that process herself.

As the spiral turns, we move next to the Autumn Equinox, the time when the light gives way to the dark. Ariadne is the Goddess of the thread that in her myth takes us through this darkness.

ARIADNE

Ariadne the Goddess of the veil and the bridge between the worlds. In Celtic mythology she is the veil Goddess of the web and threads of life.

Ariadne is also the Cretan moon Goddess of the labyrinth. Her myth is long and complicated, and I have only concentrated on a few aspects. She seems to have been the mistress of the labyrinth in Crete. Cranes danced in it, and are associated with the Goddess of Fate, the alphabet of the sacred vowels and the sounds of creation and the universe. Crete is also associated with the snake, and snakes are associated with the mysteries of the death and rebirth of the women either as part of the menstrual cycle or as part of the initiation process.

According to mythology, Ariadne became a mortal woman who helped Theseus find his way out of the labyrinth. She did this by giving him a ball of wool which he unwound as he went in and rewound as he came out after slaying the Minator. This myth seems very remote but is very close to our own mysteries. The Minator symbolizes the destructive aspect of the self, or the shadow of the self, which we have to face and discard in our lives.

The thread is part of the weaving mysteries, and joins us to the beginning and end again. Ariadne represents the force that needs to be left behind and that then goes to the next level. Like Iris she guides souls through the underworld, leading them with her thread. As she winds the thread she herself comes back to this world. The labyrinth is full of twists and turns, representing how we can get lost in our own processes. We have the choice to go to our deaths readily and face the unfaceable to find what it is that we most fear — either death or madness.

Ariadne is left behind on the island by Theseus after helping him. She is then found by Dionysius who represents the next level of the mystery. She now becomes a woman who can experience the ecstasy of life within herself. We can also celebrate the life force within our bodies and within the world, we are connected to our bodies and to the creative aspect of nature. She is the guardian of the crossroads between the meeting of death and life — the death of the monster and the meeting with the creative force of life.

Ariadne's thread is like a road, which connects her to the Celtic goddess Ellen of the Ways. Ellen is the guardian of the inner and the outer roads of life.

Like Athena, Ariadne is associated with the mask of Dionysius. In Myceanaean mythology she hangs on the tree. The tree is the symbol of the self, which is upside down as she hangs on the tree. We have to go through the doorway to find ourselves the right way up again. Like Alice in Wonderland, we have to move to a different viewpoint of the world.

Robert Graves describes an image of Ariadne with a black egg.[6] It is from this egg that we are reborn to start the next cycle of the mysteries. If it is true, as C. Downing suggests, that when Ariadne hanged herself she was pregnant, it would suggest that the baby was born in the other world, or the next phase of existence. Here we are truly born again to start the next cycle of the spiral of the labyrinth. We are neither truly dead nor truly alive. Ariadne is the Goddess who lets the threads down between the worlds, and it is along this thread that we can travel to the other layers of the spiral.

With Ariadne we learn how we can use the wool that we have spun to travel with. We can learn to make it into patterns to live our lives by and to unravel these patterns so that we can start again. It is with her that we can learn the steps of the dance that takes us into an ecstatic trance so that we can see the other worlds and find the place to which we are to journey next within ourselves. It is interesting with Ariadne that she was left behind on the island for the next stage of her journey instead of travelling. It is as if she had to learn to sit still for the next person in her life to enter.

To sit still in this place of the abyss is an important stage of the women's mystery process. It is as the Goddess that we sit over the abyss and allow the space for things to come to us. It is like a web or a net with which we are waiting for our next catch. In this phase we learn to allow the next thing to manifest in our lives just by sitting still and being so that we can make space for it to enter. Hence the abyss is the place of space. It is not always necessary to be doing something; sometimes just sitting still is all that is required in the right frame of mind. The labyrinth is the key to the other world. It is the key pattern that has to be woven into our lives so that we can go through the doorway into the otherworld of our soul. The rebirth of the next level is the crossing of the lesser abyss and moving to the next ring of the spiral to the time of the Beltane festival on 1 May.

MAIA

Maia is the great Weaving Mother. Her name is now given to the month of May. This is the time of the heliacal rising of the Pleiades (Seven Sisters). In pre-Christian times the 1st of May was the time of the Beltane festival. In England this festival was associated with maypole dancing and other festivals to the Goddess. It is also associated with the making of a sacred fire and with the cooking of cakes within that fire. The maypole is a large tree sometimes living and at other times cut down, which is used by the community to represent the living spirit of the earth. It is brought into the village on May Day, stripped of all its branches, and decorated with flowers and ribbons. The ribbons are long and in the colours of the Goddess, and used in a weaving dance around the pole. People are divided into two groups, traditionally male and female. One group goes clockwise, the other counterclockwise, in a weaving pattern formed by the ribbons. This represents the powers of the stars or the sun shining into the earth and making the crops and trees fruitful for the summer.

F. McNeill[7] gives an example of how the need fire of Beltane was made by nine groups of nine men rubbing two pieces of oak together in relays until the virgin flame of the rising sun was sparked. This gave the appearance of the flame coming straight from the sun.

McNeill says (p 63) that roks and spindles were commonly made of rowan wood. It is recorded that an old woman who lived in Selkirk in the mid nineteenth century would regularly every Beltane procure a new rowan tree pin, which served her as a talisman for the next 12 months. The rowan is the tree of the

Goddess, with its white flowers, red berries and dark bark. Rowan trees may have been used for maypoles because they are attractors of lightning. This would suggest that they attract the powers of the heavens and bring them down to earth, which is what people are doing in the maypole dancing. The red berries are like the food of the Gods in Europe, and may symbolize menstruation as red food is often taboo and the food of the dead. The rowan or mountain ash is also known as the quickening tree or the lady of the mountain. Robert Graves gives it the name of Luis, meaning brilliance, glory blaze. Its name may be derived from the root of the word red or wheel. The Gaelic word for spinning wheels is *roks*, and both spinning wheels and spindles were traditionally made from rowan. The three fiery arrows of Brigit were said to be made of rowan. K. Naddair[8] suggests that the rowan is the Celtic tree of life, and like other trees of life would probably be guarded by a serpent.

The mysteries of Maia seem to be connected with the union of male and female, the two different aspects of the universe that can create life. Although most of the Goddesses in the cycle of the spiral seem to have been self-creating originally, after this time there was a union of opposites at certain times of the year: the dark and the light. Beltane is the end of the dark and the beginning of the light. These two principles are seen together at this time before the other takes over. It is a time of the light in the darkness and the darkness in the light, like the Taoist symbol of yin and yang.

This was the time of balance when union could take place. The Goddess would either come down from the sky or up from the earth and meet with the God. A sacrifice was usually made at this time for the marriage to be completed. After this union the Goddess would become pregnant, and the cycle would continue. Her pregnancy brought fruitfulness to the earth.

Although the union is physical in the myth, it is also an inner union. It is called the mystic marriage, and is an important part of the alchemical tradition in which the new king and queen lie together as part of the formation of the gold. By including sex in the festival, those participating can gain an understanding of sex as a sacred act to the Goddess — an element missing in the relationships of today. Sex is a sacred act, with many more layers to it than physical pleasure. It is part of the divine mystery of life.

Maia is both the crone and the maiden, showing the connection of the cycle of the mothers and the change of the seasons. Beltane is a celebration of the earth changing its mantle, becoming veiled in the green of the leaves from the brown of the branches and the earth. She is the mother of the weaving the beguiling of love that traditionally happens in the summer, and the weaving of the energies that allow us to follow the lead of the mother at this time of year. She is not the Goddess of love like Aphrodite, but rather the Creatrix like Eros, who creates the energy for love to happen.

The close connection of Maia to both the hag and the maiden shows that she is both life-giving and life-taking. This is the time when the maiden would become pregnant with life. It is the time when the Goddess has returned from the other world of darkness to give forth life and bring the fertility back to the earth after its rest during the winter months. In our society we now understand that way that the earth cycle goes in terms of how nature is fertile. By being in contact with the seasons and celebrating them, we can reconnect with the earth and its cycles both within ourselves and on the earth. This is very strong form of sympathetic magic.

The red berries of the rowan reiterate the idea of this being a change over time between the crone and the maiden, the berries being the fruit of the other world like the pomegranate of Persephone, the flowers being the flowers of the maiden Goddess, and the bark being the dye of the crone. It is also a time of change both within the body as the Goddess becomes pregnant, and because the flower is very much like the eye or vesica symbol, which is the shape we travel through to go to the other worlds.

Here the Goddess moves to another level of understanding within ourselves in that we go around the cycle again but this time with the growing child within and the growing of the earth. We are growing the new self on this journey: a self that we have formed with our own knowledge and in the image of the self that we want, free from the influences of others. This is the time of rekindling the virgin flame, the flame of the mysteries of the light in the darkness, the flame of the Goddess.

Here we start the second level of the spiral but this time as a Priestess of the Goddess, since it is the Priestesses of the Goddess that keep the sacred fires of the Goddess. She is represented by the fires in her temples, and becomes that spark of light that creates the life of the Goddess. At this time she is carrying the fire in her womb, which is born at the Lammas festival in August.

The great weaving of Maia is the weaving of the maypole and the weaving of the life force down into the darkness. The light of the sun is then carried to the next festival of Lammas on 1 August. This is the time when the sun is waning and the light is going into the ground preparing for winter. Arianrhod represents this as the Goddess of the Spinning Castle of the Stars.

ARIANRHOD

Here we move to the time of birth, of life and death — the death of the king but the birth of the sun/son. This is the time when the wheel of fortune spins and we find our destiny for this life. The spinning wheel is like the crown, and Arianrhod is associated with both the crown and the spinning wheel. The crown is like the halo and the circle of the aura; it is the circle of gold around the body and the head. It is also like the wreaths of flowers or laurel that the Goddess wore at the times of festivals.

Again it is the time of the maiden and the crone, with the making of the corn dolly or the corn knots that protected the home during the winter months from the ravages of the Cailleach. The corn dolls were made in the image of the crone or the maiden, or in the form of a knot. With these knots the Cailleach could control the winds of change. Menstruating women were also thought to be able to control the weather. The association here seems to be that the weather very often changes at the times of the full and new moon and women very often have their periods at this time. According to Barbara Walker, the knots have the form of the mandala, and have been used in Celtic knotwork designs that symbolize the meeting with the God. Knots are believed to tie up the vital spirit of the person on whom the knot is placed.[9]

The knots of Celtic design can be used for meditation and to get us into a state where we can reach the realms of the Goddess and her castles in the sky, or the castles of the higher realms of our being. We can use these twisting patterns to find a way to her realms in the stars, where she gave birth to herself in the beginning of time.

The spinning wheel is the wheel of the Goddess that turns the wheel of the year or the wheel of the mill that feeds us and makes the flour for the sacred cakes. It is also the spinning wheel of the heavens, connected with the Fates, the Goddesses who controlled time and fortune. The wheel is therefore associated with the aspect of the Goddess Venus or Fortuna. Arianrhod's wheel is the silver wheel or Caer Sidi, the spinning castle of the heavens, which is both a prison and a temple of rebirth, like the womb.

Arianrhod is the queen of the night and the darkness, and the lady of the moon. She represents all that we wish to do but have to hide for fear of society. The queen of the night is the person that we are behind the veil, trying to get out, our true self. She was famous for her beauty, but locked up in a castle that only the hero could enter. But she was also an enchantress. She is the bestower of gifts to others naming and arming her son. These arms are usually the magical treasures of Britain, which she keeps for those that have earned them.

The hero's sword has two edges: one dark, the other light; one for healing, the other to kill. This is like the fates, who can give life and heal a person, or kill him. It is interesting to note that the heddle used in weaving is also known as the weaver's sword and they are very often similar in design and look, though the weaver's sword has never been sharpened. The sword has two edges and a central shaft that carries the energy, which is woven into it before the edges are used for cutting and changing. The sword is the implement that brings change.

Arianrhod is the other-worldly consort of the hero. Why does the hero need an other-worldly consort? He comes willingly to this castle to receive the knowledge of the wheel. It is the place of the fairy queen, the underworld of the Goddess from whom knowledge is received. By entering the castle it keeps it going in its spinning motion. She is the dark woman of the wheel of knowledge or the revolving spindle. She is the power aspect of ourselves. It is her that we become when we find our power and can stand alone. We then become the self-creating principle in our own lives and use that principle to guide our lives. We can initiate others into this principle by our example.

While we are in this castle, the hero enters to upset the pace of our existence. This is the person wanting initiation into the mysteries. In the story of Arianrhod it is her son who comes asking for a name or an identity, then for arms, and then for a bride. Symbolically it is the new self unfolding and asking first to be recognized, then to be given power within the self, and finally to find the relationship with another that is real.

Arianrhod is the Goddess of the Winter Solstice, when on the twelve days of Christmas the children were given presents from their mothers or the Fates for the coming of the light again. She is the challenge who has to be overcome in order to receive wisdom. One has to request to wrestle from her the sword of wisdom that can only be given to one who will truly serve.

Arianrhod is the other-worldly woman and it is from her that the sword comes. It is the sword of Fairyland forged by the spirits of that land, and when the hero dies it is to her that it is returned. The idea of women with swords is rare in mythology, but behind all the famous swords seems to be a woman. Swords are very often returned to water or another realm belonging to the Goddess.

To understand this aspect of Arianrhod you can give yourself a present for each year of your childhood. These presents should represent what you learnt during each year, being symbols for the energy that we obtained during those years. If this seems difficult, reward yourself with a present for each of the first 12 years of something that you would like now or would have liked to have had then.

In the spiral of the Weaving Goddess Arianrhod comes at the time of Samhain, the Celtic new year. There is some confusion between the old Celtic and the Christian calendars. To me she represents the light in the darkness, like the stars, and the darkest time of winter. From here we move to the next ring of the spiral: Brigit, the Goddess of the light returning, and the festival of Imbolc at the beginning of February.

BRIGIT

Brigit, like Neith (see p. 44), is the Goddess of the Fiery Arrows. There is not much difference between the arrow and the sword of Athena or Arianrhod. The arrows represent the filaments of the fleece that she spins into the wool. The fire is from the heavens or the stars being brought down to earth. The main sanctuary of Brigit was at Kildare in Ireland, and the sacred fire that was kindled there was tended by nine Priestesses to the Goddess. This sanctuary survived until the fourteenth century. The area is now the site of the Curragh — the main Irish racetrack and the home of the national stud. There is a connection between the goddess and the morse totem. Images of Brigit are made from the last sheaf of wheat cut at Lammas and saved to be used at the time of Candlemas.

Brigit is also associated with the snake. She is the great queen of the sky, now much changed by her acceptance into Christianity in the form of the Virgin Mary. She has all the symbols of the Goddess who represents the light of the stars and the universe. She is the opposite of the Goddess of the dark, who is the space or the void between the light. However, these two are really inseparable and should be seen together, as two sides of the same coin, or sword. She is like the flame in the darkness that leads us towards the light of our being, which is our goal.

This is the higher principle of the Goddess that helps us to understand our lives and path. The Goddesses at this level are the archangelic forces of the cosmos, the mediators of creation, who can help and guide us. Hence Brigit is the Goddess of smithcraft, healing and creativity. Smithcraft is a kind of alchemy. The heating and changing of metal into another form is paralleled in our lives in that we change the raw material of our birth into the steel or iron that we would like it to be. She is the Goddess of transformation and change through the heat of her fires. These are the sacred fires of change and rebirth, represented by her spindle, each loop of thread on the spindle being the reheating of the material for it to change yet again.

Brigit helps us to heal the stresses and strains of our lives, which affect our bodies and our very cells. The pollution of the earth also greatly affects our bodies, if not physically then psychically, as we are part of the living earth. Magic is about affirming this connection, and it is the severing of this connection that has made the earth and our bodies so sick. It is to Brigit's light that we have to look to find a new connection and to free ourselves so that we can become well again.

Brigit is like the Divine Sophia, the divine wisdom of the earth that has to be allowed to live so that we can continue to live and survive on this planet. We can achieve this healing by both men and women finding the true wisdom of the Goddess and allowing the wisdom of the feminine to enter our lives. This is about caring and having a relationship with the earth, ourselves and others. She is the guardian of our creativity.

Creativity is a sacred vision that we forget that we all have, but we can start to find this creativity by working with the Goddess and making images of how we see or feel her. We can then show these to others so that they can also start to find their creative vision. We can use this creative vision to help to heal the world. It is also the vision we have of ourselves in that we become the part of the creation that we have made and we can then see ourselves within it. It is the light of our spinning and weaving and the fabric that we have made. We shine as the fabric shines, and it becomes the mantle of our being and the web in which we are contained. When we spin and weave with our own creativity we can form a structure with which we can hold our inner self in safety. We can hold our own being in our own self-love so that we can be truly independent yet allow the love of another to enter and our own love to leave this container that we have created.

Our love and the love of others or another can leave and enter on the rainbow bridge. It becomes the bridge of the energies of the goddess or of what we have created. She also has a saintly aspect to her in that she is devoted to what she is doing. She is the patroness of women and the protector of women in childbirth, being a midwife. We can all be her Priestesses, tending her sacred fire by having a sacred fire in our homes. It need be no more than an altar flame that you light when you are in the house. Some shrine lights can be left burning permanently if you have a high shelf and no cats that might knock it off.

Brigit is the Goddess of the dandelion, which gives us a yellow dye — the colour of the flame of the stars and of her hair. Her season is the springtime when the lambs are born, which gives her an association with the wool used in spinning. She is also the Goddess of the green fire, which is the fire of the earth in the springtime, the shooting up of new life at the time of the return of the sun.

She also has associations with the borhan, the drum of the Celtic people. On this drum we can beat out the rhythm of life or the beat of the heart that is our pulse and the pulse of the earth. We can make sacred song on the drum so that we can celebrate the mysteries of the goddess and dance her dance until we become ecstatic. Then we can form a communication with the Goddess and receive her mysteries. She then becomes the voice of the universe speaking through us. With this rhythm we can connect with the above and the below at the same time, as the rhythm keeps us going down while we rise with the dancing.

The last goddess on this spiral is Neith, also associated with Nuit and Net in Egyptian mythology. Hers is the time of the dark and the waning sun at the time of Lammas, the time of the death or the cutting of the corn.

NEITH (NET, NUIT)

Neith is the Goddess of the dark blackness that balances the divine light, and of the void or the dark space between the stars. She is the Lady of the West, where souls go to rest. Her symbol is the arrow, like Brigit, and also the shuttle which in iconoclasm is placed on her head. Hence she is also a Goddess of weaving.

Neith is an enchantress, and her temples in ancient Egypt were associated with the mysteries of life after death. The walls of her temples were covered with scenes of what happens to the body after death. In the embalming process a piece of linen was placed in the hands of the deceased on which were painted figures of Isis and Hapi. This cloth was intended as an amulet to bring the mummy under the protection of Net, in the form of a magic knot called the *sac*. She was thought to be the protective eye looking after the body.

E. Wallis Budge gives this invocation to Net:

> Hail, mother great, not hath been uncovered thy birth!
> Hail, goddess great, within the underworld which is doubly hidden.,
> thou unknown one!
> Hail, thou divine one great, not hath been unloosed thy garment!
> O unloose they garment.
> Hail Hapt (Hidden One), not is given my way of entrance to her.
> Come, receive thou the soul of Osiris, protect it within thy two hands.[10]

Net brought the linen apparel to deck the face of Osiris, which had been woven for him by Isis and Nephthys. This apparel was of white, red, green and purple linen. The dead were embalmed in her chambers, and she oversaw these ceremonies. In her aspect as Nuit she was the sky at night, and the stars were believed to be the travelling souls of the dead. She was believed to have woven her own veil. Nuit/Nut was believed to give birth to the renewed body of the sun each morning and to protect its body during its journey through the darkness. Nut makes the vault of the heavens with Naunet in the lower realms, thus forming the great round of feminine being. This becomes the cauldron of rebirth in which the Goddess gives birth to herself and her children. This round forms the cosmic egg of birth and death, the place of rest and rebirth. She is the first sound of the universe, which starts the creation of life.

Neith is the origin of the Fates. Women connected with these mysteries are always thought to be enchantresses, able to control the fate and destiny of the soul. We saw that Isis as a healer could do this because she was the one to whom the Fates bowed.

The mysteries of death are the ultimate in mysteries, since no one really knows what they are about, although the shamans and the magicians who have travelled to this realm seem to have very similar ideas as to what they are. The mysteries of death are bout the preparation for this realm and what we may meet on our journey there. This is the movement to and from the greater abyss. It is the greatest journey that we have to make. It would seem from the way that the Egyptians prepared for this journey that they thought that by preparation we would get further along the path each time so that the journey was easier each time.

The journey is about being able to cut the ties of the last existence so that we can float freely in the vastness of space ready for the next rebirth. This floating is like resting the body, though it is the soul that rests so that it can find where it needs to go to next. Some of us find it very hard to die and others very hard to be born, and this is the barrier we are crossing when we meet this Goddess. She is our guardian until we go into the realms of light, and of this pathway between the worlds. She is the protectress and the challenger of this doorway, unlike Ariadne who is the guide and helper over the lesser abyss.

THE CENTRE

The centre is like the eye of the Goddess, and also the axis of the spindle. It is the vesica through which we pass on each stage of the journey. It is also the egg that is within. There is an egg without as well, which is the shape of the spiral. It is in here that things are gestated and start the process of growing. To leave this space we have to go out through the eye (like the eye of the needle or the loop of the Ankh). In the egg the process of alchemy takes place, and so it is the vessel of transmutation and change. As in alchemy we have to leave the vessel and burn away the residue before we can start the process again.

The eye is like the opening at the top and bottom of the world tree so it also represents the world tree axis of the Goddess. All these Goddesses have sacred trees with which they are associated. The tree has been vernerated around the world and is part of the mysteries of the Goddess. It is also a symbol of the self in that we also have branches, leaves, flowers and fruit. The Goddess is also associated with birds in that birds and other animals live in this tree. Again, all the Goddesses of this cycle are associated with birds. Animals also live in the roots of the tree and seek food from it. It is like the totem pole of the animal totems that we have in our bodies and each of the energy points. We have an eye at the top of our pole and the vagina at the bottom, the two openings through which life can form: the physical life and the soul life. Both are needed for balance in our lives.

Eggs are symbols of death and rebirth, which were placed in the burial chambers to promote rebirth and also as a symbol of birth itself. Here the connection with birds is reinforced in that it is the birds of the Goddess that lay the multi-coloured eggs of life.

Eyes form the dew of our bodies or the tears of life. The sacred trees also have tears of life from which the sacred scents of the Goddess are made. The eye is like the centre of the spiral. In many of the ancient monuments the spirals carved into the rocks are in pairs resembling eyes and energy spiralling forth. These eye-like shapes or spirals are often features of these stones, some strongly resembling the eyes of owls, a bird strongly associated with these mysteries (See Gimbutas [11]). Gimbutas[12] connects the egg with column designs within the egg, and with the shoot of the seed coming out of its casing. These columns are often in the darkness of the underground part of the temple, reminding us of seeds that sprout in the darkness, like bulbs and other spring flowers.

The Egyptians planted seeds in the sarcophagi of the dead so that when they went into the chambers it would give the impression of the body coming back to life. In the marked stones of Gavrinis, Brittany, the stones are carved with the pillar design and in the arc formation of the radiation of energy, such as comes from the new growth of a plant.

These columns could also be the snakes of the Goddess in her aspect of coming out of the earth reborn. The snake is both the spiral of the energy and the column of its central axis. Snakes also lay eggs. They sleep in spirals, change their skin and are reborn, like the losing of blood at the time of the menses. They are the guardians of the trees of life in all mythologies. They are also the emblem of death because their bite kills. In their sinuous curves they symbolize a river, the river of life in which we live, or the Milky Way snaking through the sky. The Ouroboros (the snake eating its tail) is a symbol on which the Goddess is often seen standing. It can also form a crown. The most famous snake design is the caduceus of the healers. It has been discovered recently that snake venom can cure illness, particularly MS.

The egg contains the mysteries of the Weaving Goddess. It is the shape that she has woven to enclose herself in for protection so that she may go deep inside. It is also the centre of the mystery, the eye of the needle through which we journey to different worlds. It is both the beginning and the end of the spiral. It is the symbol for the self.

2

THE PATH OF THE PRIESTESS

THE START OF THE PROCESS

I remember the day when walking in the garden after a summer thunderstorm I saw for the first time the colours of the trees, plants and the sky. They were all luminous and very alive. I was very aware of being part of this earth and that we were all connected by this luminous light that came from the earth and all living things. Seeing this vision was the start of the process of my awakening and of my connection with the plants and the trees, which has never left me.

One day I woke up and realized that my life was not quite as I wanted it; something was missing. This feeling kept recurring for several years before I really started to consider what was wrong. I knew that I wanted more from life but could not identify what. The start of the process for me was trying to find what I really wanted.

The realization that something is not quite right gives us the energy to start to do something about it and find out why. I was doing a job for years and got as far as I could within its structure and then found that as I could go no further I did not know what to do. In the end my attitude to the job became so bad that I decided that the only thing I could do was to leave and see what happened. This felt like a great risk, but I felt that if I followed this path then the path would provide what was right.

At this time I had become familiar with the idea of the void and the Goddess who sits and waits for creativity to come into her life. The waiting was four months before I saw that what I should do was to go into business for myself. As soon as this happened it all fell into place, and in my new business I was suddenly offered lots of work. This is like the spinning process. The waiting is like the carding of the wool, and the spinning the process of deciding what it was one wants, then drawing these fibres together so that the process works with all aspects of one's life. All these things are about learning about the self and the responses that one has to make to what is happening.

Learning about the self is very like the process of the Goddess Iris. She is the messenger of the Goddess, and is like a butterfly going from place to place disseminating information both for herself and for others. Without this process it is impossible to find out what it is that we really want, because as we move to different parts of the self we find that we have different needs and that these are given different levels of importance according to how we are feeling at the time.

Finding out about the Goddess is learning about the self. She is an archetype with which can all identify in some way. The myths and stories of the Goddess can give us something which we can use as pointers in our lives. The images are for later when we understand her in terms of patterns. The start of finding out about the Goddess is like opening Pandora's box — anything can come out, and we have to be prepared for this. The myths and legends of the Goddess can help your life in all sorts of ways. They work rather like fairy stories in that they stimulate the unconscious parts of the self so that a deep understanding is reached. They can also be used consciously to help solve a problem by meditating on the images within the stories to see what insights can be received from the mental images.

A story that I have found very helpful is the myth of Psyche as found in *The Golden Ass* by Apuleius,[1] written in the first century AD. It is the story of a man's initiation into the mysteries of the Goddess Isis. In the middle of this story the ass and a young woman are told a story about Psyche and Eros by a woman in a cave. It is the story of a woman and her search for the lover/God that she has lost. In a sense the woman is looking for the lost parts of herself so that she can be ready for the relationship with the Gods, her higher self and her lover. The Goddess Aphrodite, whom she resembles, sets her various tasks; the sorting of large amount of mixed seeds into their various types: obtaining some fleece from the wild rams; obtaining water from the source of the Styx high in the mountains; and going into the underworld and bringing back a jar of beauty cream from Persephone. These could be seen as the tasks of a woman in her self-discovery.

We have to sort the seeds, or the parts of the self, so that we know what is contained within the self. The seeds represent our inner potential. We can plant these seeds so that the creative spark and our potential can grow within us. We can decide which seeds to grow first and where we should plant them.

Acquiring the fleece from the rams is like acquiring knowledge to be able to plant these seeds, and continue on the path. It is learning ways to pass ideas from one person to another and gain a deeper understanding of where we are in relation to our own process.

The journey into the mountains to the source of the Styx is like the journey inward. It is the countryside we first meet when we start journeying into our inner landscapes. It is the hardest part of the journey in that it is here that we meet all the blocks and resistances for the first time — which we will meet over and over again on the rest of the journey. Meeting them for the first time is the point when we are most likely to give up as we do not have the knowledge of how we overcame them before to help us through the gaps within these obstacles.

Going into the underworld to fetch the jar of beauty cream is the journey to find the inner energy to go on this quest and to fight the obstacles. These underworld journeys come when the obstacles are at their strongest, when we give up all hope and move into darkest parts of the self and the depths of despair. It is here that we can find the answers so that the journey can continue. We can also get trapped in this place.

In these tasks Psyche has various helpers. The ants come and sort the seeds for her. Ants represent the mind's capacity to select one thing from another. This principle often works intuitively in our lives so that we select as we move on. The whispering reeds help her with the fleece, advising her to sit and wait until the sun goes down to collect the fleece. This is the function of the feminine: to wait until the time is right before we can continue with a task. It can only be done in the time of the twilight when we are between the worlds and in contact with both the conscious and the unconscious. Next it is the turn of the eagle to come to her aid. The eagle represents our spiritual principles soaring above us. It is only with the aid of the highest ideals that some tasks can be achieved. They come to our aid when the going is the most difficult and we most need the help of our inner resources. These inner resources often come to us in our dreams and other visions as solutions to problems that we are having.

Psyche's journey into the realm of the Goddess Persephone is another journey in itself. It starts with her wanting to give up and jump off the tower. The journey takes her along the Styx into the underworld realms and then past the Goddesses of Fate as they spin and weave, to the Temple of Persephone to get the jar of cream. This journey in its essence shows that we have to be very concentrated in our task if we are to complete it. We have to keep our vision straight forward, otherwise the energy which we need to continue with the journey will be dissipated by distractions.

This is also the realm of the Cutting Goddess. When we have finished a task we have to cut ourselves away from it. We have nurtured the project, and now it must now grow by itself. Giving up emotional attachment is very difficult, but it is here that the Weaving Goddess can help in that with each death comes the rebirth of another project after a period of rest. This knowledge alone can sometimes help us to continue. A word of warning, however, is that when you are really concentrating on a project and it is working well, all sorts of things will start to happen to test whether you can stick to the path, and to help you go through the levels that the path necessitates at this stage.

All journeys involve the changing of something if they are worth following. That is the nature of an inner journey: to find out more about the self and to move onto a different level of understanding as to what the self is. With each level we go deeper and deeper into the self and closer and closer to the divine within and without.

OPENING TO HIGHER POWERS AND TO SEE OTHERS

This is the next stage of the journey, when we have some idea who we are and what we want, and now want to go further. This is the part of the journey where we go and find others who have also taken the journey, and are looking for others to share their experiences with. At this point we can go and find what is available in the local community. Some say this is the hardest part of the journey, others find it easier. However, sharing the path with others gives support to our individual journeys, and their experiences can give us help with ours.

This is very important as in this society we do not have this type of training as a norm, so we have no reference points in the way that we live our lives. It is not a part of our teachings as it was in ancient times. At the mysteries at Eleusis, according to reports, thousands came to the ceremonies. It was considered a good thing to go through this type of initiation with others.

In the story of the Golden Ass there was a journey to the sea, a ritual drama and the unfolding of the mystery, all of which took several days to complete. It was held in two parts, the lesser mysteries in February and the greater mysteries in the Autumn, at the Equinox. It was a rite of passage, in which the whole society took part.

The path of the Goddess no longer has such a large following, but her mysteries have, and are always celebrated somewhere near to you. The mysteries have taken other forms at different times as the needs of society have changed, but they are still the mysteries of the Goddess. In the Dark Ages the voice of the Goddess was heard through the Christian mystics and nuns. In later times her mysteries were just visible in the Hermetic strands of the occult schools. They are also part of the Marian cult, and were present in Gnosticism in the form of Sophia.

Group celebration of our spiritual natures is very much part of the human way of doing things. We have always met together in groups to celebrate the divine in ourselves and in nature. There are examples of this from all around the world, in all cultures at all times. (See Joseph Cambell.[2]) This can be seen from paintings and writings throughout the ages.

Finding all-women groups nowadays to celebrate women's mysteries is more difficult, as it is a more unusual aspect of the Goddess and of religion in general. There have always been groups of women that have celebrated the mysteries together without men; evidence of this can be found in myth and legend. Brigit had Priestesses who tended her sacred fire. At another sacred fire were the Priestesses of Vesta. In the other world are the Priestesses of Avalon. Finding these sorts of groups nowadays is more difficult as the shrines are not usually public knowledge. However, most occult bookshops sell magazines, and through the contacts that these have you should eventually find the sort of group that you are looking for. This is an outer quest in that you have to go out and actively seek the sort of group that you want to join. Don't forget to ask friends, because most groups get members through the recommendation of friends.

Religion is a very personal matter and the formation of groups is very important, so whoever enters the group has a very strong effect. People are therefore quite careful of who they choose to join groups. Another way to find people is to go to occult conferences, which are advertised in magazines. There are also courses organised by various organizations, which are advertised in the classified sections. Courses are a good place to meet others of a like mind.

THE SORROWS OF THE GODDESS/HEALING THE HURTS AND THE WOUNDS

The sorrows of the path are when things die or have to be given up in order to continue with the path. The saddest example of this is the sorrow of Isis when Horus died and she had to bring him back to life, and when she had to find the slain parts of the God Osiris, which had been scattered. In our lives we have to go through this process over and over again. We have all felt loss at some time in our lives. Probably the most difficult losses are those of death or separation. The death of a person that one loves is a very powerful emotional experience; one is affected on all levels at once and often without warning.

One of the aspects of the Weaving Goddess is endings, and as the Goddess of Death it is she who decides when a life is ended. This understanding can only really occur when a death has been experienced. It is when you have this connection with both worlds that you can fully understand the dying of the leaves in the autumn, knowing that growth will occur again in the spring. The annual death and rebirth of the tree is easier to accept because the cycle is short.

Working with the Goddess of Death we can begin to feel that this too is the process at work. The process does not replace the mourning period, which is an essential part of bereavement. The death of a person is much more complicated both because of the emotions involved and because the idea of rebirth has to be taken on trust — in the inner process and in the Goddess. At the time of death she often shows herself so that the feeling is confirmed on an inner level.

Healing the hurt or the wound of death is much more difficult, because this has to be both a group experience and a personal, inner experience. Healing can be achieved with the help of the Goddess both through ritual and meditation. The rituals at the time of death are very important and should contain within them the chance to cut the cord or the threads that connect you to the deceased. If this cannot happen within the ritual at the burial, then it can be performed alone in your own way. To do this alone you need to be able to think clearly about the person who has died. It does not have to be immediately after the ceremony of death but can be at any time that feels right to you, even years later. If you are thinking clearly the ceremony will come to you, though it might take several days or weeks for it to come right. Trust in your inner voice to tell you what to do. It need not be very complicated; an acknowledgement to the inner self is enough.

A very emotionally painful form of death that women have to work with is that of abortion or miscarriage. To me this is not the death of a person but of an unformed creative spirit within ourselves. I feel abortion is a very personal decision and should be accepted as such. Only the pregnant woman can decide if that is what she wants to do. However, if an abortion is felt to be the right decision, then a ritual to the spirit of that creation can be a great help to relieve any guilt and to reform the whole again after the invasion of the operation.

Ritual to aborted fetus

Light candles to the unformed spirit of creation and allow these to burn down without going out. Say your goodbyes to what could not happen. Add any other feelings to the candles that you want to leave at the same time, like anger, perhaps at the person who caused the pregnancy. Remember to get rid of anger at yourself as well and allow all these feelings to burn away. Soon afterwards plant a tree or long-lasting plant so that although this life could not happen another can.

With people the rituals are usually more personal in that they are to do directly with the person and your relationship to that person. It is very difficult to give guidelines as they should be personal to the people taking part in the ritual and the person that has died. Some guidelines that I would suggest are to remember to add your negative feelings as well as positive feelings to the ceremony, as these are part of the reality. Do not be afraid of disapproval. Allow it to be a celebration of the new life that the person might lead. Talk about the feelings that you have for that person and how you will miss not being able to have these feelings any longer. Celebrate what the person achieved in this life.

When people, plants or animals are very ill, these illnesses need some extra energy to help them to recover. Here the Goddess of Fate can help in that by doing a healing for someone you are spinning more energy for them into the weaving of their life. Healing is like mending or darning a worn piece of the cloth of another person's life. This is usually a very difficult process in that the amount of energy and the way that it is woven have to be similar to the cloth already in place. With practice this becomes easier and easier.

The best way of contacting the patient's cloth of life is by getting their breathing and your own into harmony. Keep this going for a while, and then allow the energy to rise in the rhythm of this breathing. When it has reached its height, allow it to enter the body in the same rhythm. Always be watchful in case the patient's breathing pattern changes as the healing continues — it often does.

More specific healing might need other things added as well. If there is a disease then the patient will need to have a very clear image of what this disease looks like and how it is going to leave the body. If the patient is too ill to do this by meditation close to the patient, this can be felt but should be checked with the patient if possible to see if it resonates. The healing energy can then be added to aid this process and to make the images stronger. Art and image-making are very useful here. With animals and plants you have to find the part of yourself that links with the disease and then find mental and visual images from there. In group healing everyone should have the same visual image to concentrate on as this helps focus the energy on the same point.

Energy rising is the process of the Fates *par excellence*. It is the spinning of the energy as it is raised through breathing up the energy of the earth and down the energy of the stars. It is also done chanting the vowels that are the sacred sounds and letters of the Fates, and then weaving this healing energy into a thread that can be woven into the person or thing that needs to be healed.

When the weaving is completed, then the thread that has been woven needs to be cut. This cutting should be done very carefully so that it is not a shock to the patient or the healer. The entry and exit of the healing energy can be a shock to the body of the patient. If the cutting is not completed thoroughly, then the patient may unconsciously go on tapping the new source of energy and your own personal energy may be drained. This occurs especially if you were not fully fit yourself when the healing was performed, as you might have been unconsciously looking for some healing for youself. This identification with the patient is enough for the link to be made.

Cutting the ties in a parting or relationship break-up

This is very hard to do, but can be very beneficial if the boundaries become much clearer and there is no confusion. It is best done with the person that you want to separate from, but this is not always possible. The ritual should be tailored to suit individual needs but could contain the following elements: the actual cutting of a cord; time-span to allow the parting to happen (one month to one year). The form of words should show the connectiveness of life but the need for these two lives to be separate at this time. Within the prescribed time limit some sort of change should occur in the relationship. You should also acknowledge the good things that occurred in the relationship and the things that you learnt from it, phrased in the most positive way possible. This is important as it puts very positive energy into the ritual.

THE CAVE OF THE GODDESS

This can be the place that you go to after the cutting or the splitting. It is the place of rest and recovery while waiting for the next project to enter into life. It is the place to go when you feel that your energy has been drained by the day's work or events, or when you need to cut off from events around you. This is the cave or the place of mysteries of the Goddess. In her darkness you can recharge your batteries so that you can face the next part of the journey. We all need to find or imagine this place. It is a sanctuary from the interruptions of the world. We can create this place in our minds either out of our imagination or from a place that we know and alter it to suit the imagination.

Real places are good for inspiration. Visiting the sites of the Goddess is very much part of the mysteries for me, both to see the sort of places that were used before and to use them as ideas for visualization. Interesting caves that I have visited are the Long Barrow at West Kennet and the chambers at the Hyperiogeum in Malta. These are not strictly caves but they are places of darkness, and the chamber in the Hyperiogeum is associated with the Sleeping Goddess and the receiving of inspiration through dreams. There is also a large cave at Tintagel in Cornwall.

If you combine all these places together you end up with a cave of your own design. Having a place to retreat to is very important. In this space you can find the sacred, hidden parts of yourself that make up your being. It is not really a place that you go to to be active in but rather a place of rest where you can get recharged. It is a place of waiting while in rest. It is a place of stillness. The world and life still continue, but you are resting and waiting for the time to be active again. You are waiting for the creative spark that comes and sets you going again.

In the story of Ariadne it was Dionysus who was the spark of her rebirth and moved her on to the next level of existence. She did not have a cave but travelled to another island. In the story of Psyche she herself kindled the light that set her on the journey to find her true self. First she was in the darkness and then the light arrived. It is this light that is often associated with the mysteries of the Goddess. When she makes herself manifest she is like the light in the darkness or at the end of the tunnel.

This place of waiting is like the void or chaos, and these words originally had the same meaning. It is a place of nothingness like darkness or the sky on a dark night. In the nothingness you know that there are things around, but you cannot see them clearly. You are content with the unseen, as not being able to see is restful and allows you just to be.

It takes quite a lot of practice to be in this space as it is so unlike our normal being. In our society we are constantly bombarded with images and sounds, so we have forgotten what stillness and silence are. It can now feel very dangerous to go into this place of nothingness and just be. We are sitting on the throne of the Goddess when we are in this space. We are almost united with the Goddess in her dark and unformed being. We are like the seed in the ground in winter: the seed is alive, but it is waiting for the warmth of the spring to start the process of growth. When we have learnt to be in this space, it is from here that we can receive divine inspiration, and see the light in the darkness to lead us forwards.

This space has a negative side in that it can also be the place of depression, seeming like a prison from which there is no exit. We can go here and feel trapped — that life is not worth living and that we are not worthwhile enough as people to try to leave this place. It is as if all that we are is worth nothing. It is like being trapped in the labyrinth of Ariadne. It seems that the passages are labyrinthine and that you are just going round and around in circles, and that there is no exit. You have lost the thread of your being.

All the stages of the process of becoming a Priestess have their negative side. Because this is one of the three great transition points of the spiral, it is one of the most difficult to get out of. When in this trapped or imprisoned state the best way to get out is not to panic but to try to work towards becoming calm, to learn to relax in this place and become at home in it. As soon as I feel OK being there I find hope again and the light returns.

GOING OVER THE ABYSS

The care of the Goddess can become very womb-like and feel very safe so that we do not really want to move from it. This can be the cause of the depression: we want to stay yet know that the time has come for us to move on. This time can be very painful as we have the information that we thought we wanted, but we are beginning to see that this is the start of the journey not the end. We have to go on as this becomes a stronger and stronger yearning from inside. The light that we see in the cave can be what takes us across this boundary; so can the urge to change the situation that we find ourself in. Strong emotion can also stimulate us to go across. When we have arrived on the other side we know inside that something has changed. There might also be an outer manifestation of this, perhaps in work. You can also make a conscious decision that your life needs to change and that you want to bring another level into your life to find something that is missing.

Working with the Goddess's energy you may find either that it takes you to another level in your life or that it shows you the possibility, which you may like to find for yourself. The different sides or guises of the Goddess found in different cultures are an indication of this process of change. Very often as you move through and work with the different aspects you can see the various levels which you can attain. She can speak to you from afar, and then you realize that she can also speak to you from within as you develop this process. The process can then move on so that she can speak through you to others who need her advice. All these are aspects of the same process of going through the levels of the Goddess and the self. This is the first big step on the path to becoming a Priestess in that a belief that she is there within and without known by your whole being is very important and the start of the further journey to the Goddess.

The Goddess is the all-protecting mother to the followers of her path but she is also the great challenger. It is the challenges that she throws up that really cause us to change and transform. That is why following her path is even more complex and difficult than not to do it. I have also found that the challenges often come up during one of the festivals and that these are the hardest challenges to resolve, as they are connected to this sacred time and have to be dealt with in accordance with the time of year and the seasons, and take many months to resolve.

REBIRTH OF THE SELF AND THE CHILD OF THE GODDESS

When you come out of the tunnel and see the light and brightness of the new day's sun it feels like a rebirth. Shamans talk of this experience as if they have been in the depths of the earth and are rebuilt by the powers that reside there. They talk of the spine being remade and hollowed out. This is very like receiving the sword of the Goddess, which is placed within one's back so that one can have the powers of cutting and pruning that this weapon can give. This process can be done either by conscious effort or by accident. Near Death Experiences come into this category. A strong experience happens to you, and when you come through it you are changed and life can never be the same again. Most of us have had this experience, which is different for everyone.

Life at present is a challenge for us both individually and as a society. I believe we have reached an abyss and how we get over this point is going to affect those that come after us in a way that no society has ever faced before. We need to be like the Goddess Maia and give birth to a self that can inspire us to move on and to inspire those that follow. We have to be able to find this inspiration from within as we are not receiving it at present from society, which has lost touch with its vision of the feminine. This is shown most clearly in the way that it has lost touch with nature.

The rebirth of the self is like the birth of a child. In some cases the birth of a child here can be negative in that we can give birth to another in the hope that they will take the process onward where we have given up because we are frightened of leaving the security of the known. However, giving birth can equally be the process that takes us onward.

The reborn self is the sacred child, the divine inspirer within. It is the part of ourselves that is going to take the light into the darkness and see the unseeable so that we can find and understand the process in all its aspects. In alchemy it is like going to find the lady Venus and lifting her veil. We go and look upon the process of creation within ourselves so that we can see that we are alive and that we do have some part in this creation process. There are stories of how the Goddess while in the cave during this time of darkness wove the mantle of the heavens that covered the universe.

As we are reborn we come out from under this cloak so that we can view the process from a different angle. We are the ones who form the mantle and also the ones who lift it so that we can go behind. We form the sleeping Venus from our lives and we weave the mantle that protects her. We then have to awaken that part of ourselves so that it can give birth to the new self. It can become the spring and the mantle of flowers that covers the earth with new life. This awakening birth-giving process will lead us forward into the other realms of our being, and to the understanding of our part in the process of life.

We are forming and creating all the time. This will give us a guide as to how the process is happening and a direction and purpose so that we can see the path ahead and why we are following it. This is the formation of the self that is in the twilight zone, the self that is neither fully conscious nor unconscious. The creative part can feel the lead of the conscious and the unconscious. It is aware of the decisions that have been made, and of how they were made. It is part of that process, but it is not necessary for the self to assume full control as its role is as the advisor or the mediator intervening when something is going wrong, giving advice so that this problem need not occur again. The hard lesson that the newly forming self has to learn is that it cannot control these unconscious and conscious processes; it can only aid, advise and support.

At the start of this journey, we create the sleeping part of ourselves behind the veil that we have woven in order that we can go back to find it again. When we first start this journey to see the upper levels, they may be overpowering as we have not yet formed a strong enough self to contain these parts within ourselves. We have to start by forming the container and the boundaries in which we can receive this spirit, and then it can enter our bodies. This means that we have to look after our bodies by keeping reasonably fit and by examining our mental processes to form a true mental picture of what our values are and how we function within these morals of our own making. If this container is not woven to the right specifications and to our correct needs, the spirit will not be able to enter and we will feel that we are constantly looking for something that should be within but is still without. We can feel it trying to get in, but we can't find the door to let it in.

The new-born self is the child of the Goddess who resides within us, and is also the new self that is forming within the container that we have made for it. When we are ready we can look upon this being and see the real self, a powerful experience that can result in another death. We will either become that person and start the refining process again or will die and start again, as this was not what we wanted or we could not cope with it.

GROWING WITH THE GODDESS

The new spirit of the Goddess has entered us, and we are beginning to feel her presence and know that it is with us at all times. She can now be called upon at all times to give us advice. Her words of wisdom come to us through our dreams and in our meditations. We can travel to her temple in our inner vision. We are in contact with the inner spirit that is forming within us. It is like the process of getting to know a new friend. Like all friendships, it is complicated and difficult, and we have to work at it. As with totem animals, we need to make contact with it often for its full value to be realized. To continue this contact it is often necessary to formalize the contact procedure. This can be done with formal meditation procedures.

Once we have found the road to her sacred temple, we get to know the landscape within which we are travelling, noticing the familiar landmarks along the way and any buildings or unusual trees. We then see the doorway into her sacred precinct. This is not necessarily a building; it could be a grove, the sea-shore or a cave. When we have reached the entrance-way into her temple we have to learn the way to gain access. This can be by the permission of a guardian through the making of a special signal at the door. In this case the signal will be given through meditations on the door. We may need a key, which we have to search for. Another being might bring it. When we go through the doorway we have to find the way to the inner temple of the Goddess. Here we may have a guide, as in the Chymical Wedding of alchemy, or we may be allowed to explore alone. This depends on the type of contact you have. Some are not Gods or Goddesses and will have their own temples and courts where they all meet. If the contact is a Goddess she will have her own temple, but if she is part of a pantheon the others will be close by.

The type of contact that you have with the feminine principle will depend on the sort of work that you have done previously. I have had no formal occult training, so my contact with the Goddess has been alone and in places that resonate with me. When I have worked with others, this contact has often been more of the collective kind in that there were others in the temple and often more than one higher principle present when I arrived.

Magical groups often have a contact with the Goddess which comes from the group mind. This sort of contact would not necessarily be considered to be the Goddess and could be seen as a totally different higher principle. My experience of this type of contact, whether called by a male or female name, has a very feminine feel and is very much part of the feminine mysteries in that she often comes through the female members of the group. I have found this to be a very powerful part of the mysteries in that you receive the spirit of the group through yourself and you speak of her mysteries.

Communication with fairies is different from with totem beasts or ancestor spirits, and different again from the contact with beings that have some sort of human form, but they are all creatures of the Goddess. They all speak with her divine voice to the various parts of ourselves, and give messages that we need to receive in all sorts of ways at different times.

The Goddess gives us various tests at different times during the course of our studies. These are like the tests that Arianrhod gave to her son, who had to find a name in order to receive his weapons. The giving of names and weapons is the prerogative of the Goddess. It is from her that these gifts are received and to her that these gifts have to be given back. As in the legend of Arthur and the Lady of the Lake, she gives him the sword of the realm and when he died he has to return it to her before he can go to the other world and await rebirth. She can also be very testing in the way that you enter her service. The more dedicated you become, the more changes you have to deal with, often several at once.

The transformation of the flower bride is part of this process; she is the personification of that which is formed by another, who wants her to be something. She decides, however, that she wants to control her own destiny, and is then transformed into the owl, a sacred bird of the Goddess. As a bird of the night it could be seen as a negative side of the feminine. This transformation is the crossing of the next abyss in that she becomes who she wants to be and is now a woman unto herself. She has the spark of herself and the spark of the Goddess both growing within.

The flower bride is the rebellious part of all of us. She wants to be the centre of her own world that she has chosen and created for herself, not one that has been created by another or by the society that we live in. We too want to have the power of our own choices. We can then go out into the world with confidence that these are our own choices and that we are therefore going to be successful. This will bring healing to ourselves and to others.

GOING OVER THE GREATER ABYSS

When we have found this inner knowledge and wisdom, we need to go out into the world and share this with others. It is very much part of the journey to do this, and confirms the inner knowledge we have found. Often when talking to others we find they have had similar experiences. This confirms our own inner experience. It is this inner and outer process that is the crossing of the abyss, the ridge of darkness that we find within. It is crossing from the darkness of creation to the light of the manifest. It is the act of crossing that forms the world that we want.

We make a rainbow bridge so that we can go backwards and forwards as we please. But every time we go over this bridge we are changed in some way and the world becomes slightly different. We cannot make the journey without this change, as it is the change of the Goddess going from one aspect to another. There are four of these bridges that connect one phase to another. They all go from the centre to the next phase but can be taken in any order. They make the spiral pattern of change in the world. As we move around the bridges we form the spiral but we also make it move. The motion is continued each time we move over the bridge. The spindle makes more thread, the weaving grows, and the shears cut the thread. The veil is lowered and rises again. Life moves on and we continue the path of life, of creation and death.

The spaces between the periods of action are very important, as these are the times of rest and also the times of recharging our batteries. As we move over these spaces we are creating the spark that will light the flame that is the energy for the next phase. It is important to realize this, as without these times of being in the darkness we do not have the energy to go on and bring our inner wisdom out into the light.

CREATIVITY AND THE FLAME OF THE GODDESS

The flame of the Goddess is the perpetual flame associated with worship, that is kept constantly burning her Priestesses. This flame is always within us and lights our path as we journey forwards. All the Goddesses that I have discussed have a festival of lights. In their light that we see in the darkness that comes to us when we are despairing at the last minute. It is her who leads us on to find the creative being that is within us.

We are all original creative beings, and the marks that we make are original to ourselves. Only we can make these exact marks. This is the spirit of ourselves in contact with the Goddess, with the energy of the creation within our own being. All around the world images of the Goddess are made that are a representation both of her creative energy and the creative energy of the maker. She inspires us to be creative and it is with this creativity that we are able to find the movement forwards in our lives. She is the inspirer of the Navajo sand paintings in America. These paintings are made individually each time for the patient that is to be cured. They are inspired both by the patient's illness and the Shaman who is doing the healing, and also by the spirits of the earth that are represented in the painting. This is the creativity of the Goddess in her healing form.

Music and the chanting of the Goddess are also used. These are the healing words of the Goddess that come on the winds; the sacred vowels or the alphabet that is carried in the bag of Athena; the sounds that come from the underworld or the darkness to be sung in the other worlds; the sounds of the breath of life sung in the other worlds. They bring these worlds to life and are the stimulation for the other worlds to go into a mode of creation. This creation comes from all the worlds simultaneously working together.

This is the time when profound vision comes and our lives feel as though they are working in harmony, all together at the same moment. We feel the energy of the universe pulsing through out body. We feel the earth in motion, spinning, weaving and cutting all at once. This is like the potter's creation of the pot or the weaver's creation of the basket; all the aspects of the Goddess are present at one time.

If and when we can all move together, we can find an inner harmony and peace within ourselves. We are in contact with ourselves, and we are also out with the energy and moving with others. I feel that we have to establish our hearth within ourself and within our physical environment. We can then enter and leave this hearth as we please. The process of moving in and out then becomes like a spiralling as we move around the hearth, like the planet Venus of the pentagram. Then, as these spiral pentagrams form next to one another, we form the weaving of the sacred shape of the body of the Goddess. This is why we form the images of the Goddess: they are like totems of the process that we are going through.

Some of the shapes that are found on the carpets of the Middle East are the universal shapes of the Goddess. They are the refining of this process of working with the Goddess down to its simplest yet most profound form. Marija Gimbutas in *The Language of the Goddess*[3] uses these shapes to show how the language of the Goddess has been put into her icons and her symbols. The v-shape, the zig-zag and the spiral are the most common. There are also the snake, the net or veil of the Goddess, as well as the egg and the tree of the Goddess. All are part of her mystery and the representation of this mystery. At its simplest it can represent all life. The spiral is the spiral of life and the eyes of the Goddess. The zig-zags and the v-shapes are the weaving. The net or veil is the cutting and the moving to the next phase. The tree is the axis of the spindle, the warp of the weaving, and the shears closed after cutting.

The triangle or yoni is the shape from which all life comes and to which all life is returned. The triangle represents the creativity of Brigit and the light with which the creativity is inspired. Brigit is the Goddess of healing, smithcraft and poetry. She combines all the skills of the Goddess, like the divine Sophia. It is in these skills that we can form and transform all of our being. Like her, we are all and everything. Smithcraft is the heat of transformation, the fire of the alchemist's flask in which the transformation can take place. It is the heat of her light that we feel when the process is working well. The energy changes as the work progresses; it goes from being totally obsessive to not being able to be finished. All this is the process of the Changing Goddess, part of being in contact with the origins of the creative process within ourselves.

The flame within can be found through meditation, with the aid of ritual and the shamanic form of going on a journey to find the light or the spark of the original creativity.

ALONE WITH THE SELF, THE GODDESS, AND THE CYCLE OF LIFE

This is the phase where we are in the total light of the Goddess, the desert of her creation. It is the place from where we are able to see all, but it is very difficult to be original as here we have to work with what we have already created. We are very likely to go into burn-out in this phase, as here we labour to finish the work that we have created. We add the gems of our own creation that make the work shine in the light of the sun. The iridescence is in the weaving of the cloth. The place of the desert is the place where we are alone with the Goddess. We have gone there voluntarily in order to find wisdom from the light of our being; to communicate with the Gods and to find the wisdom from the upper realms. Here the wisdom is very like the information that we receive from the contact with the Goddess, but it is more direct, as we sit and wait for this information to come through. The Goddess talks to us directly in the form of a vision, but before we arrive in the desert we have to be able to survive the light of the sun. It is the true light of the solar principle which shines in the outer world and in our being.

THE EYE OR THE TRIANGLE AT THE CENTRE

This is the place that the spark comes from, the hole through which we come at the time of birth. It is the eye of the needle through which the thread of life is threaded so that we can embroider the pattern of our lives. We embroider the pattern, but we are also responsible for the weaving of the cloth and the spinning of the thread. This is the start and the finish of our journey as Priestesses, and even though we can start this journey anywhere the centre or the eye is the place to which we keep returning.

Very often the journey starts in one of the places of the abyss, either the dark prison or the desert of the light. Being here either moves us toward the dark or toward the light. This is the journey to find both the dark and the light, and the twilight is the twilight of vision, where we can see and use the energy of both places.

The eye at the centre is the Iris, the start and the finish of the journey, as are all the Goddesses that we have discussed in this cycle. Every process has a beginning and an end. The path of the Priestess repeats this process over and over again, yet with each repetition of the journey we move away and yet closer to the hearth of our being, the temple of our own making. This is the centre of our own mandala, the image of ourselves from which the parts of our being radiate in an every outward and every inward spiral.

The eye at the centre of the mandala is the very essence of our being. Drawing mandalas is a very good way to recontact the centre of our being when we feel that we have got lost in the process of our own creation. Mandalas are like the centre of Ariadne's labyrinth. When we are at the centre we have the

67

thread, so we can find our way out again. Mandalas are usually divided into four with a central point; they are then subdivided as the circles spiral outward. But they can be drawn in any way that feels right at the time, and their creation is an important part of the mystery of the Goddess.

3

WEAVING THE CLOTH OF THE WORLD

The realm of the Goddess can be divided into three worlds with a fourth surrounding them. These are: 1) the upper world of light, represented by the Virgin of Light; 2) the middle world of the twilight, represented by the Red Queen; 3) the dark world of the night, with the Dark Duchess. There is also the world of the Noble Empress, the light in the darkness representing the whole or the world of balance (see Figures 5–6).

THE GOLDEN WORLD OF THE LIGHT

This is the conscious world of daylight, the visible, waking world. It is the world of the predictable where we feel that we have control over our lives. It brings heat and light into our realm of existence. The light of the day is the manifestation of the creative force. It is believed to come from the east and the dawning of the sun of the new day. It is the realm in which the Goddesses live, and the light of the sun is the light of the Goddess. It is the realm of the archetypes. The archetypes are the forces that are simultaneously at work in nature and in humanity. They are the first principles, which govern the forces and the pattern so life. These are the patterns that make the weaving.

The light is the opposite principle to darkness. These two form a split that we as humans try to integrate. The coming together of the dark and the light forms the pattern and the balance of life.

We try to release the light in the darkness. Some people only relate to the world of light, and all they find within is darkness. This is because they have not also found the light in the darkness.

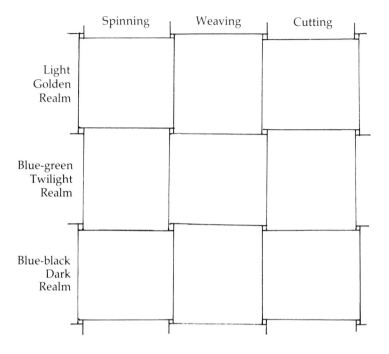

Figure 5 *The realms of the Goddess and their colours*

It is from this realm that the Goddesses talk to us and we hear their messages. It is the realm to which we travel to meet with the Gods or the higher parts of ourselves. This is the world from which we receive the divine inspiration of life. Contact with this world can be very difficult in that when it is reached the archetype can take us over and we have to live out the wishes of the Goddess in the world. We feel that we are driven by their messages and that these have to be fulfilled. This can be both negative and positive. For some it can provide the divine inspiration that is necessary to live a fulfilled life; for others it can seem like a demonic contact. Both forms can come from this realm of the light, the stars or the sun in the sky.

THE TWILIGHT WORLD

This is the world of transformation and change. It is the world of the dawn and the twilight. It is a magical realm that is very much

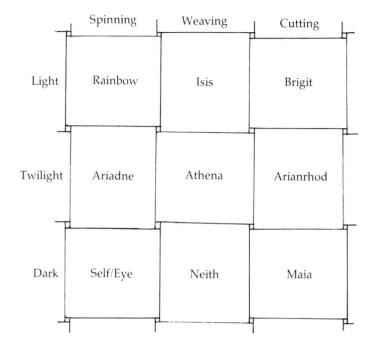

Figure 6 *The realms of the Goddess and their representative Goddesses*

part of the countries of higher altitudes. In countries nearer the equator there is no twilight. The twilight world is a time of magic when the world loses its hard edges. It is the world of the rain-storm and of mists and fogs. It is very much to do with water and the transformations that occur when water is moving or changing. Dew is the water of the dawn, the rains and waters of the heavens, and the fogs, the mists of the earth mixing with the heat of the firmament. It is at these times that magic takes place: the magic of going into the light or moving into the darkness.

To go from one to another one has to pass over the abyss. It is the place of the mixing of both worlds, it is the doorway or hall of the palaces of the Goddesses of both the upper worlds and the underworlds. It is the time when the sun and the moon are often visible together, when changes can happen in the cycle of the year. It is the times of Beltane and Samhain, when the veil of the world is at its thinnest and we can travel to the other worlds.

At these times it is best to meditate either early in the morning or in the early evening — or both for the dedicated. This is when we receive the wisdom of initiation and the dreams that help this process to unfold. In this realm we can travel across the waters to the other worlds and learn their knowledge and wisdom. These are the worlds in which the teachers live. They are the worlds in which healing can take place.

These are the realms of Avalon and Lyonesse the places from where the great heroines came. They are still accessible at this time if we choose to journey to them. These realms also contain the realms of the monsters and the land of women for the more courageous traveller. Like the golden realm of the light, the twilight has its negative side. You can go to this realm and never leave, for instance if you eat the food of the fairies. You can be lured to stay and never come back, or not fully, because they are the realm of eternal youth. You end up with the feeling of living half in one world and half in another, and that nothing is really real. This can be avoided by careful travelling and attention to the myths associated with a particular realm.

THE REALM OF THE DARK

This is the realm of the concrete and the realm of darkness and night. It is the place that the emotions come from as well as the realm that gives us the inspiration to continue the path and the quest. The dark world is like the compost heap in the garden. The plants and the trees are in the realm of twilight or waters, and the golden world of light is the realm of the flowers. The dark or blue-black world is the realm where the cutter has her home. However, this is not the underworld of the Goddess, which is the realm of the yoni and the cosmos and is the place within which all these worlds are manifested.

The dark earth is the realm where things grow and also decompose, the place of solution and dissolution. It is very difficult to see as it is so intangible; in a way nothing happens here, yet everything happens here. This is the place of the food for all the other realms, and it is very close to the world of the underworld were the forces of challenge are located.

This is the place that the foundations of the other worlds are built on and from which they derive their strength. In this world we are decomposed and then the new shoots sprout. It is the winter resting place of the leaves and branches before they shoot again in the spring. It is the dark earth or the *prima materia* of the alchemists. This is the substance from which gold is made by refining it in the realm of the waters where the gold of the upper world is formed. It is the place of the dark moon, of the magic of the night, of the meeting at the cross-roads with the forces that cause decomposition, of the spirits that live deep within the earth. These ancient spirits dwell in the realms of chaos. They are the energies of original nature, which formed itself from the void of nothing into the world of being. These are the basic creation spirits that form everything from within their dark mass.

In this world, as in the compost heap, can live several 'nasties' or 'creepy-crawlies', but they are harmless. It is our fears and fantasies that make them into our enemies when they could and should be our friends. The world of the darkness is very much about learning to rest and allowing things to form in their own time, like nature, which waits for the heat of the sun before starting the process of growth. It is also about truly relaxing into the realm of darkness so that the process of decomposing can take place. So the dreams of what we want to be can be found in the darkness, and we can form the next stage of the process.

THE MATRIX OF THE GODDESS

All these levels weave together to form the weaving of the Goddesses of Fate. Weaving together the threads they make a three-by-three pattern of nine; this is the pattern of the weaving, formed by the integration of the spinning, weaving and cutting with the worlds of the dark blue, the green and the gold. The colours associated with the Goddess and the Moon are black, white and red. Red and green are opposites but the same principle; white and gold are also joined; dark blue and black are the colours of the night. These make the nine squares of the goddess: the five of the elements from which we and she are made, and the four of her four phases. They are the squares of the dark and the light, which together make the sacred numbers of the Goddess. Here we have the magic square of the goddess, and within this we can manifest all that we require in the way of transformation of the self.

The three-by-three square is the magic square of Saturn, who is also the ancient mother Bindar, mother of chaos and of the void. In later times she became Saturn the time-keeper. All the mysteries of women are connected with time: the cycle of the moon and women's menstrual cycle were the first clock or calendar of the world. It was also her who sat in the primordial chaos and waited for the right moment to start the process of creation. Each of the squares contains within it the energy of a spirit of change.

SPINNING GOLD

This is the formation of the golden rays that penetrate the world of the green and the world of the dark blue. They are the showers of golden light that impregnate us in the darkness. They are the messages of the Gods coming down to earth and giving us the seeds from which we can start the transformation process, which we sow to start major new events in our lives. It is like the thread of life that connects the spirit body to the physical body. It is the shiny thread that connects us to the astral. It is the golden thread that is woven to make the crown of the stars. It is the golden thread of love that connects us all to the sacred web of the universe, that makes us all one in the world. We are all part of this web or net. We are each a star in the cosmic net or the veil of the stars. It is the thread of the umbilical cord that connects us to the Great Mother. It is the thread of DNA, which carries the genes of future and past generations. It is the thread of life, and we are the living representations of this thread. It is the winding serpent around the Tree of Life, which gives us the choice of individuation. It is the sacred cord of the Goddess. It is the cycle of the earth around the sun through the zodiac, which makes the spiral of life.

All these are the golden threads that are woven on the rainbow of being. When a rainbow if formed, the sun shine into the darkness and passes through the watery realms to form the prism of light. The light divides into a spectrum, to show the seven sacred colours of life or the rainbow. These are the seven energy centres of the body, the seven planets of the visible world, the seven pillars of the wisdom of Sophia, and the seven stages of the alchemical process. All are contained within the golden thread, which has seven strands.

In magic this golden thread is like the gold that threads through the earth. It is the golden seam that miners hope to find, the image of our own golden seam within. It is the channel through which energies can flow. The thread wraps itself around the axis of the spindle. The golden threads are like the snake around the Tree of Life, which is the divine guardian of the apples of the trees. These are the fruits of immortality. We have to grow our own golden fruits of immortality on this tree.

THE GREEN OR THE RED THREAD

This is the thread of Ariadne, which she lent to Theseus in the labyrinth so that he could find his way out of the maze. It is the thread that is woven into her crown of flowers. It is the thread that leads us through the darkness of our being so that we may find the true image of ourself, like our own reflection in a mirror or a pool of darkness. It is the thread that we need to carry with us at all times so that we may if necessary find our way out when we are lost. It is the thread of blood that moves within the whole human race. It is the cord that Isis wears around her waist to show that she has found her connection to both the past and the future. The green thread is the thread of the plant world, which feeds us and runs through the sacred plants and trees of the forest. It is the thread of life that we eat and that forms the cells of our bodies. It is the cord or thread that forms the cloth from which we clothe ourselves and with which we make the baskets to carry the food back to our resting places.

SPINNING THE DARK BLUE

This is where we spin in hope. It is the putting of the thread through the needle. We don't know where it is going to end up, but we still twist the thread and put it through the eye. We work in hope and trust. We are working towards a process, in trust that we will find what we are looking for. It does not come with the end goal but with the realizations that we have while we are on this path. We learn that we can live in the everyday world but not in the future. Each day contains within it the essence of all days; it is cyclical like one moon cycle and one year. Knowing this can help us stay in the moment. Time starts to slow down when we are in contact with all our feelings. We know when something in us is blocked, and can remove the block before it becomes connected with the blocks of the past and can only be removed with difficulty.

This is the place of being in touch with the process of life. We can relax and know that what the future brings is not important as we are in touch with the feelings of the present and we can live the dream of our lives. We wake each morning and can work with the dreams of the night. This is the place of these dreams. In the mysteries it is one of the most important sources of inspiration that we can have.

Spinning is the planning and the making of ideas that span all the worlds, and working with those plans on a daily basis to see if they will work before putting them into a long-term plan.

WEAVING IN THE LIGHT

This is the weaving of Isis at the death of Osiris. Isis and her sister Nephthys wove the shroud at his death so that their love for him could be seen in the upper realms. The weaving of these mantles is like what C. Downing did as the work of her life: presented it to the Goddess. The work of Isis was to transform the body of her lover and perhaps her own animus. By doing this she transformed herself. It was the work of her life and she gave this away to the Goddess. It is the work of the higher self and when this has been finished it has to be given away, so it may be used by all.

This is why the process of the weaving is so important, as we need to know that it was in the process that we received the knowledge to finish the task so that other work can be stimulated by the work that we finished. When we weave a creation for others, it is very important that this work is done for humanity. Very often this work is done in the darkness of the cave or by our own hearth, with no one around. We work alone driven by some unknown force that seems to know what is happening. When we don't know what is happening, we work with hope, and faith that all will be well in the end. It is this work that we bring out of the darkness and present to the Goddess and to all other women in the hope that they will no longer feel alone and that the inner journey we have been through will be of support to them.

By this process we hope to heal ourselves and others. By healing ourselves we help to heal the world. If we think of ourselves as a cell and we all try to heal our own cell, then the whole world starts to become healthier as good health spreads throughout the whole body. Some do not think that the world is sick or that it needs healing, but I find that what we have done as a race has given the earth a psychosomatic illness. The surface skin of the world is very polluted and the rivers are not only running low but are full of poison. The sea, the place of creation of our being, is full of our poison. Fish are no longer the messengers of the unconscious with a life and being of their own, but a food crop. This is the sort of energy waste that we have to watch. By healing ourselves and finding what our own needs are we can help the earth sustain itself by only taking from it what we need and by giving back the healing and health that we receive from these gifts.

WEAVING IN THE TWILIGHT

This is the weaving of the garments of change, the cloak of invisibility, the mantles of healing and the mats of prayer. These are the clothes that can change our lives. We use the mantle of invisibility when we need to rest and regenerate our energies, and do not wish to be disturbed. We also use it when we don't want to be seen by unwanted kinds of energy, when we travel to the other world for the healing of others. The mantle should not be used to hide from things that we do not want to face.

This is the mantle of the Goddess. In visions she is seen with this mantle of dark blue around her, like wings that can surround us and made us feel comforted and secure. This is the cloak of change that shamans use when they travel to the other worlds. In the women's mysteries the Swan maidens wear a famous cloak of feathers which they take off to bathe. There are also the salmon-skin hats worn by the creatures of the sea, and the cowhides worn by the land shamans. When wearing these garments it is easier to transform into an animal shape and travel to the worlds that these creatures inhabit. Today it is not really possible to have a cloak of swan feathers as our thinking on this level is very different from the ancients, but it is possible to weave or to embroider a cloak like this, containing the spirit of our wish to journey to the other worlds.

We can also weave our own mat of prayer, to be used every time we meditate or work. It is the sitting place of our power and we have woven this intention into it so that we can trust that the journey that we go on while we are sitting on the mat will be safe and well. These mantles and mats are like the stars wrapping themselves around us. They keep us warm and give us protection.

WEAVING IN THE DARKNESS

This is going into the void, sitting and manifesting all that we want in our lives. The void is the place that many fear to go to, it is the place of the darkness that is within us all. It is not a negative space or a place of depression or a prison, but a place of darkness, where there is very little light apart from the light of our own being. Here we can rest from the world and just be. We are aware of time, and of our feelings, and we are very alive, yet we are at peace. It is the place where we can manifest the being that we want. We can also manifest things for others, although this should not be done without some thought as it can be a drain on our energies in the lighter worlds. What we do in the darkness has a very strong effect on the other worlds of our being, as this is the seed of the three worlds and the energy for others' worlds. To manifest in the darkness is very simple: you go to this space and see if what you want is possible from this space. If it is, it will happen, and will manifest in the other worlds as well.

The results will be given in the form of gold in the golden realm. You need to go to the darkness to seek permission for this. If it is possible, then a light will arise from within your being at this point. If you don't know what you want but are trying to find out, then the dark realm is the place to go and to see what you can manifest. It is rather like a meditation. You can also go to the darkness through a ritual journey. You can choose the method of access to suit yourself.

For myself I achieve this state by both means. In meditation I have made a journey to the dark realm by going down into a cave or dark place and then leaving through a tunnel at the other end, passing through the realms of the stars, to a place that is dark and is not inhabited by any stars. I suspend myself there and see then what comes past me. I am suspended there by the filament of my own being. It is like being in a net that I have woven for myself.

In ritual I have reached this place of darkness. I have then looked deeper and deeper into the darkness. The ritual has involved moving in closer and closer to a cauldron in which the mystery is contained. Along the way I have had several challenges as to why I want to take this journey and what I want to obtain from taking this journey. These challenges come from the others taking part in the ritual. The part that I have played is the traveller. I have also played the part of the guide for others who wish to take this journey.

This journey takes us into the inner realms of manifestation and of our being. When we get to this place we have to wait and see what happens. This is often the most difficult part of the journey, when the fears and disturbances of the everyday world enter our sacred space. These are the first of the disturbances that we have to work with, before the space becomes the quiet place of peace. They are very normal and can come at any point in the journey, no matter how many times you have made the trip. I often find that I encounter the spontaneous fears of that particular day, which can give me very strong insights into the emotions and thoughts that I have had during that day. Sometimes they indicate things that have happened during the day which I have missed, for example, when I have been confused in a meeting and have not really understood what was going on. Then in the meditation an image, often frightening, has come up that has explained the inner working of that meeting. Often I gain an insight into what I can do or what could be achieved in a certain situation.

This is the power of the dark world that I call the void, because at the time of entering it there is nothing except my presence in it. This causes things to enter the void, like a light attracting a moth. The moth is the inspiration for that time; its colours and patterning are the patterning and the colours for that time. If you get nothing from a particular meditation, try using the image of a moth attracted to a candle flame. See if this image can give you the inspiration you need.

It is similar to doing a meditation outdoors; nothing might come other than the peace of the space. If this happens, when you open your eyes the first thing that you see can be the answer to the question. The other directions can be the finer details to fill out the answer. This sort of magic is very simple. What is around you can give you the answers; it not need be any more difficult than that. If we open our eyes, we can see, and all will be revealed. Answers are never very far away.

CUTTING IN THE LIGHT

This is the giving of our creation to the Goddess. We do this when we have finished the process and are ready to give it to others and so let go of what we have already achieved, making the space to move on to something else. Every so often we need to clear out all the ideas that we did not complete, so that this again allows room for further thoughts. It is a good idea to give these half-formed ideas to the Goddess so that they can go back to the realm of chaos for others to use. I find that I have far more ideas than I can possibly use. Storing them for future use just clogs up the mind and makes it feel over-full, and exerts a lot of pressure because all these ideas are pressing for attention. These excess thoughts and ideas have to be given away in the realm of the gold and not anywhere else; then they will go back directly to the Goddess.

This is a process worth working with when a project becomes stuck. It is like starting again but from a different place. It is devotion to the cause or to the project which allows this to happen, as well as trusting the process so that it can happen in its own way and in its own time. When we do this we are working with the true energy of the higher self, which understands the path that we are walking. The Goddess helps us but we have to go over and over the ground so that a full understanding of its potential can be found. We need overview after overview to understand at the deeper levels. This is not the only way; sometimes we can just study one thing and go steadily deeper all the time.

CUTTING IN THE TWILIGHT

This is the moment we decide that we have studied a subject sufficiently to reward ourselves with the tool of that study. In mythology this would be the gaining of a token from the Goddess. It is interesting to note that in most mythologies it is the Goddess that gives these gifts, very often as a result of a conflict or a struggle that she has instigated or a battle that she has caused. This is her form of testing. She is asking us to prove that we are worthy of her gift. I feel that we can and should, as women, give these gifts to ourselves. I often consciously decide to do this and then in a dream I am given a gift. These gifts are often surprising. I have been given a silver bracelet. I was given a turtle in a dream at a time when I was starting a new project. This is the symbol of the earth and it was like being given the stability or the foundation on which the work could continue. In the same dream I was also given a rose, which was like what I was trying to achieve. I have also been given a paint-box full of very bright colours. As an artist these are the tools of my trade, and so are very much to do with the work that I do on both an inner and an outer level.

When this sort of confirmation occurs I know that something very important is happening and that I really have achieved something in my life. In the dream of the turtle the vision symbolized both the beginning and the end of the process, the complete circle of being. These are the inner tools that support the outer work and give the work a feeling of completeness so that we know that the process is not just in the mind. This is the realm of the twilight vision, because it is the confirmation of the outer world and the inner at the same time.

Being given these gifts in the dream is like receiving your own magical tools in the mundane world. The tradition is that you first make the tool of the earth or the hidden woman. In the weaving system this would be the making of your own mantle or cloak. You are given the tool of the west in the traditional system, which is the cup. With the weaver it is the scissors. You acquire the tool of the south, the loom, or the weaving. You find the tool of the east or the spindle, our magical wand. You could ask a rowan tree for the gift of one of its branches so that you can make a spindle from it. You might also find a holed stone to use as its weight. Other objects associated with the Weaving Goddess are the comb and the mirror.

The realm of the twilight is where you receive these gifts in ritual or meditation. This can be done by writing a ritual of the tool that you would like to receive and then performing it with others. You are then publicly stating this need. Research is needed to understand the symbol further. Doing this research can help the ideas that the symbol contains to enter our minds further. Sometimes while we are doing research a synchronicity with the symbol happens. For example, someone gives you the symbol without knowing what you are researching.

Here are some ideas for research into the comb.

Ritual and research for the ritual of the comb

Cirlot says: 'There is a close connection between the comb and the rowing boat. It is the attribute of the mermaid and other fabulous sea creatures. There is a relationship between the comb and tail of a fish.'

Combs are rather like fish bones. We comb tangles out of our hair so that the energy flows. Combs can be used rather like a feather for the free flowing of energy. Von Franz says that hair is a source of magic power. Hair grows like the energy of the body. Combing the hair is like the ordering of thoughts.

The ritual of the comb could therefore involve going into the depths of the sea to find the comb and bringing it up to the twilight world to control the flow of energies. It could be used in healing where the energy has become blocked. In weaving, the comb is used to pack the weaving tight. Here it has a similar use in forming the weaving into a tight and strong cloth. The comb is also associated with shears, and they are often pictured together. Examples are the Pictish symbol stones and the story of Killock and Olwen. In the twilight the scissors cut the fibres so that the energy may flow freely along the strands of the hair or the thread.

CUTTING IN THE DARKNESS

This is the place to cut the ties that bind us to others. It is where we can sit and decide which influences in our life we no longer need. It is like the alchemical process of calculation in which you burn away all the old and unnecessary material and are just left with the essential material. This is a very difficult process to do. I am never sure that I have got rid of the right things, but I have found that by getting rid of everything the most important elements stay within the ash to be transformed into the next stage of the journey. Here we have to trust again, that the Goddess or the higher principle of ourselves is going to look after us and that all will be well.

This is the realm of the bonfires of the autumn, when we burn all the dead leaves into ash so that in the spring they can be reformed into new growth. Every so often we need these fires so that we can once again see our lives clearly and be able to make decisions so we can move on with our lives. This is the light we can form in the darkness, and it is in the darkness of our being that we have to form these fires. In autumn everything dies and the earth is ploughed so that we can see the true earth and contact the *prima materia* of our lives again. In the same way we should clear our lives with the cleansing fires of transformation, ready for new creation.

The chair of the mysteries in this realm is the birth chair of women's mysteries, the sacred throne of creation. It is the place that we come to sit when we want inspiration in our lives. It is made of the branches of the two world trees, the tree of memory and the tree of forgetfulness, which have beneath them the well of forgetfulness and remembrance. On this seat is the place of the creation of the world, the world of our being. The branches join together to form the sacred space or the void of the mysteries. Hanging from the forward branches is the veil, behind which creation takes place. It is to this inner place that we as women have to travel and wait for the time that creation can take place within. This is a very active phase as creation takes a lot of energy and effort. However, it is not a place for going out and doing things, as it is the sort of creation in which one has to just sit and be, in a form of active waiting for things to happen in their own time. Creation can only take place when the veil of creation is cleared by having the fire of cleansing within the sacred space.

Many women's mysteries had a fire constantly burning. The fire burnt away all the unnecessary dross and left only the refined matter from which the next stage of creation can take place. This fire is the substance of the self, which is constantly changing and transforming, never static. When we are in this place we can allow this transformation to occur. We sit in the chair of creation within the void of the stars or the void of the earth. This is really the same place in that what is above is also below and the journey to this place can be either through going up and then coming down, which is my preferred method, or going down and then coming up.

The chair spans the abyss across all the worlds, rather like the milky way. It is like the tripod that the Pythonesses at Dephi sat on to give their oracles. It spans all the worlds so that we can receive visions from each one, and see into them simultaneously. We go into this place of darkness and wait until the light of creation comes. It is like a flame within the darkness. From this flame we can see the process of creation forming. We are behind the veil. Once the process of creation has started, we go back through the veil into the world of light and then we wait and see it manifest.

This sounds easy, and it can be though at other times it can be very difficult to achieve. The time has to be right. You have to make the effort, and also make sure that you are truly free to allow the next stage of the process to happen. When this process is happening in a group, progress can be very slow, as all have to be ready before the next stage can take place. Alone it is also difficult, as you may feel ready but the time to do the work is never forthcoming. Sit and wait. When the time is right you will know, and often be given a sign.

In this darkness we bring forth the light of creation, which is in the centre of the earth. We then have to join this with the light of the stars for the magical energy to form. This is the spinning, and then the weaving of creation. It is the mixing of this energy with the light of the stars which causes spontaneous creation; this is the magical energy of the work. We can celebrate this creation with song and dance and thus help the formation of this energy within our bodies. It also mixes the energy with that of the different worlds. It breathes the breath of light into that which we have created. What we have created at this time is unknown; we have to wait and see what will manifest.

Sometimes in the mysteries we can spend too much time within the world of creation, and we then need to go out and receive what we have formed. We have to give our energy to this creation process, but we also have to be able to receive what we have formed. This can be difficult as we have to accept responsibility for what we have formed. Here again we are sitting on the throne and receiving what we have formed. We look at it with the light of darkness and see it in its true form as it is seen from behind the veil.

THE WEAVING OF THE CLOTH

The dark and the light squares

These represent both the giving and the receiving of the energy. It is the formation and the manifestation of the magic. The squares can also be the different sorts of magic that are available for us to follow. The three levels are the types of quest for this inner wisdom. There are the group quests of the light world, the inner quests of the dark worlds, and the transformations of the twilight world.

Group magic in the light world usually consists of energy creation to find and contact the archetypal world of the Goddess, and the light of this realm. It is often associated with the mysteries of the sun and the contact with the higher self. This includes both the ceremonial and the devotional aspects of the Goddess path. Rituals in this realm can be to do with the worship of the Goddess in all her forms using her idols and her sacred symbols.

In the dark realms are the mysteries of birth and death, meditation on these forms and the mysteries of the moon. These mysteries are to do with the continuous cycle of flux and change. These are the usual areas of women's mysteries in that they connect very much to the bodies of women. However, the other levels are also part of the mysteries of the Goddess and can be best used when conjoined with the mysteries of the darkness.

It is a common belief that the feminine is dark and the masculine is light. This is the true source of these energies. The freeing of this energy needs to be done in the opposite world so that a connection is made between the light and the dark. Making this connection is like plugging in an electric light and switching the energy flows so the connection can be formed. Then the light in the darkness joins with the darkness in the light. This creates the motion of the universe which would not happen without this conjoining process.

The light and the dark squares of weaving represent this relationship. The dark is below the light and the light is below the dark, and the threads weave up and down throughout the length of the cloth. The delicate balance of the light and the dark weaving would not be possible without this relationship. So at different times we will be working with the same principle, but alternately with the dark and the light energy of each. From this we get a view of the depth of what we are doing; we see it from all sides.

From this we can form the magic carpet of the Goddess, which is the foundation of the work that we are doing. As the threads go over and under the weft threads, this secures the energy. When finished the weaving needs to be cut and tied. The patterns are secured within the weaving.

The motion of weaving can be very repetitious. The action of the hands in the darkness can learn to become free, so the mind can travel to the other worlds of our being and see how these patterns can form themselves in these worlds. Through the holding of these patterns repeatedly in the mind we can see how they fit into the patterns of our consciousness. As these patterns repeat throughout the carpet or the weaving we can see that they move and change as the work continues. This represents the process of our own changing, like the patterns. These patterns become the patterns of the magic that we work with the Goddess's energy.

We can form the pattern of the rainbow magic, the magic of seeing the astral body of a person, the creation of colour within our world. When the light of the dark and the dark of the light meet, a prism of colour is formed from their joining. Here we have the colours of the plants that dye the weaving and the colours of the aura that surrounds us. The creation of this colour in our lives is very important and gives rise to certain emotions. We can recreate these feelings by having these colours around us.

We can make our ball of wool and then journey through the labyrinth to find the hidden parts of ourselves. This can be both a frightening and fascinating process. Walking to the centre of our being is very hard, as we do not really want to know what we look like. It is also very interesting as to do it we have to remove our blocks.

We can use the eye of the needle to go through the veil. The needle is the tool that can work on both sides of the cloth. It can sew the jewels to the veil so that it shimmers in the light. The eye of the needle is the meeting point of the dark and the light; through it the energy of the weaving of the two comes out and can be placed into the cloth. It is the entry and exit point of the energy. It is the tool that embroiders the inner side of the cloth, which is luminous, and the outer which is dull. This gives rise to the dark Goddess who is the shining one.

They are the great magical transformations from one thing into another of which the story of the Golden Ass is the best known example. The hero of the story is trapped in animal form, and a woman transforms him back into a person again. This is an allegory that before gaining knowledge one feels stupid, but afterwards one awakens in human form. The frog princess is another example of this. This symbolizes the change into being a Priestess or Priest of the Goddess.

In the magic of the mask we find our inner monster and learn to wear it as a mask that we can take off when we are not threatened or in danger. Here we learn to wear both the dark and the light mask of our being. This is very important to learn, so that we can recognize what mode we are in at which times. For a long time I wore the dark mask and never let anyone see my vulnerable side. This was a mistake, as you cannot expect to be understood if people can only ever see part of you as a person. Athena wears two masks; Medusa and the priestess of Wisdom.

The magic of the movement of light in the darkness is seen in the movement of the flying shuttle through the weaving. This is like the magic of the moon and the way it changes as the days change. It moves through the sky like the shuttle moves through the darkness. I love watching the seasons change as the moon changes position in the sky. It feels right to celebrate these mysteries at night when the moon is at her brightest in the darkness and to be part of her changes with her.

There is also the magic of birth: the birth of a new season and the birth of a new human being. This is the spinning of new light into the body of the Goddess and into the earth. The rebirth of the earth in the spring is the most amazing time of the whole year. Suddenly, almost without us noticing, nature starts to stir; it seems to have an inner prompting all of its own. Out of nothing the new growth is seen, and the flowers of this growth come to light to celebrate this mystery. At this time the image of the Goddess is made and is carried into the house so that the new life of nature enters the house. It is the time of cleansing, the cleaning out of the old and replacing it with the new.

There is also the magic of the collecting and the making of the magical weapons of the Goddess; the making of the bag from which all magic can be done; the empowering of magical objects so that magic can be performed. This focuses energy so that when work needs to be done this energy can be tapped. The focus or the channel that has already been made can be found and used again. We can make our bags from anything for the magical ceremony. In my magical bag I have a holed stone for work when I require healing energy. Stones can be charged with a particular energy from a holy well or a stone circle. I have a Druid bell to be used for cleansing and realigning auras, and various ribbons and water crayons for use in healing and in the making of talismans. I have a set of jewellery that I only use in ritual, a bottle of rescue remedy and some wool thread. These objects change as my interest in things changes.

I find that dancing is one of the most magical things that I do. It takes me into ecstasy as I move in rhythm with the Goddess. I can dance the dance of the universe when it breathes in time with the world. We can do the dance of the earth, the skies and the cosmos. Circle dancing recreates this sort of energy and is like the circling of the spiralling cosmos.

The worlds of the golden, the green and the dark are part of both our everyday lives and our sleeping lives; they are also present in the other worlds. In a way they are like divisions of the day and night; they are outside mundane reality yet also part of it. If we open our eyes, we can see and be part of this reality as well. Our world then begins to acquire a form and a structure that we ourselves can make part of our lives, but this only comes through working with these concepts.

The energy can create, and it is this energy that we work with in a group. The energy is the sum of the part plus the whole. When we work alone, it is what we are plus what we give out that is the magic. In the group it is the whole of the group that creates the magic. It is this at-oneness, that gives us a part and a purpose in life. We can see that we are at one with life and the universe. We can then feel that we are a cell in the planet earth. We can feel that what we do in this cell has an effect on all the other cells around us and that these cells affect others.

From this magic we can gain the power to be. We can then relax and allow life to unfold around us with the knowledge that we are being both creative and restful; that we are all and nothing. Magic is the foundation of this process. It is for the benefit of all that it is done, not for the benefit of the one.

Magic and transformation of the self will only work if we do it for all of humanity in the feeling of love and not for ourselves alone. We work through all these worlds and archetypes and learn the knowledge so that this understanding can come to us. We also need to keep in contact with this deep inner knowledge so that we can continue with the process of the celebration of the cycles of the earth. At one level they are festivals of the changing seasons but at another are the deeper contact with the being of the creation of the cosmos. As the seasons change and spin, so the worlds in which we live change and spin and we move together in harmony, with an inner and outer motion. This inner and outer harmony keeps the world turning and alive.

4

THE WILD WOMAN
OF THE FOREST

Life on earth is an interconnected web. This web is now in tatters and we need to reweave it so that interconnectedness can be found again. We need to regrow the forest of the earth again. At one time this was her web: the trunks formed the axis of the web, and the branches were connecting threads. The forests of the world were at one time all connected, but now these connections no longer exist. Through the trees and the winds the different parts of the world could communicate. This idea seems very strange at the moment because so few trees remain — a possibility almost beyond imagination. Yet at one time the earth was covered with trees, and even the deserts were once plains covered with fruit and nut trees. The deserts have been formed since the appearance of man; they were not there at the beginning.

Trees are homes for millions of insects. For instance, a tree in the Peruvian jungle was found to support 43 species of ant. Forests contain the greatest diversity of plant life, and there are still new species of plant and animal to be discovered. These are already disappearing as more and more forest is converted to commercial farming methods. Yet the forests could support both food and animals if we farmed with with a holistic and web-like approach. This would mean changes to our diet because we would have to start eating foods native to our own country. It would mean not less but different foods. Food would have regional differences, and we would not find the same food in New York as in London and Sydney. By growing and eating the foods local to our area, we are starting to form a connection with nature again, because we are connecting with the environment that we live in.

It is this reconnection that we have to find as we start to plant

Figure 7 *Representation of the Weaving Goddess on a donkey*

trees, enabling their branches to reconnect again. We start to be part of the forest expressive of this reconnection. Go out into the forest and see how many animals there are. How do the trees of the forest support these animals and plants? How do these animals and plants benefit and support the trees? See how they help to compost the leaves, form other essential chemicals for the trees, and how trees derive nourishment from these essential trace elements. There is a symbiotic relationship between all the life forms that lie in the forest. This is the sort of relationship that we could be building up between humanity and nature: we can feed and house the Goddess as she does us.

In the European tradition the spirit of this relationship is represented by the Green Woman or Wild Woman of the Forest. In art her image is principally seen in medieval tapestry. With the Green Man she represents the Spirit of the Forest. She is the principle that interconnects the Spirit of Nature with the human spirit. The word 'spirit' comes from the same root as 'breath'? (The Greek word *pneuma* meant breath or spirit as did the Latin word *anima*.) She is the archetype of the forest and the human being breathing together. We need to reach a state of being where we can all breathe together, so that we have one breath in constant motion, the spinning motion — that is the spinning of the spindle of the planet within the cosmos. This is the sort of relationship that is needed within the world so that we can all live together in harmony.

The Green Woman is the paradigm of this sort of relationship. She is the spirit of the human in touch with the essential energy of nature.In a Swiss tapestry in the Victoria and Albert Museum[1] she is shown dressed in a fleece or — hairy covering, and as a hairy being with her hands, feet, knees, breasts and face uncovered. She is often pictured with the animals of the forest surrounding her. Here we find a correlation with the feminine mysteries, because the animals are those that are associated with the Goddesses of the Web: a unicorn, lions or cat-like creatures, rabbits, dragons, horned animals such as deer, pigs, dogs, birds; also flowering trees and shrubs.

Kaledon Naddiar in *Inner Celtia* (no.7) examines several of these tapestries, including one from Vienna that pictures the Weaving Goddess on a donkey or ass (Figure 7). She describes it as: 'a magnificent portrayal of the faery Goddess, who is the fate Goddess spinning out the threads of destiny, with her magical birds on her back; her inspiration-giving cauldron slung behind; her monkey cat perched in front and some of her totemic animals all around.'

To me she is the Woman of the Forest, the fourth aspect of the Weaving Goddess. She has found and learnt to work with her totem animals and is free to spin and weave as she chooses. Her existence in a medieval tapestry suggests that her tradition was still alive at this time.

The Wild Woman is the woman who goes to live in the forest in order to find her relationship with the trees, the plants and the animals. She goes and lives in the desert, where she learns about the mysteries of the elements. She forms an intimate relationship with them so that she can use the dynamics for healing. City dwellers exist in an urban jungle which is in touch neither with the creativity of the forest nor the elemental nature of the desert. However, the urban environment has its own magical feel: these things are there but in a very transformed way. So now we also have to develop a form of urban shamanism to enable us to survive in this new environment.[2] There are several ways that this can be done. The Feng-Shui experts have converted rivers into roads and boats into cars.

In magic we often work for a large part of the week, so our magic has to fit around this schedule, but we also have to make our spiritual belief an integral part of the work that we do. We have to make allowances for the technical advances that have come into this world and see if these can become part of the magic. The word processor is not environmentally sound but saves time. The washing machine and other kitchen gadgets also give us more time.

How do we integrate this into our magic? Are 'stereos' part of the mysteries or should we use live music? When I work in groups, I like to use live music made by the group, but on my own I use the stereo a lot. Do we need to be in constant contact with nature? I think not, our lives having changed so much, but we do need some contact to restore the balance.

We cannot easily go back to a time when we did not have these technological advances, but we could use these resources better. This is what we should be working towards. To go totally 'back to nature' is impossible, greater harmony with the planet is possible. This harmony comes from being in her realm in all her aspects — being outside not only when the sun is shining but experiencing the wind and the rain as well. We have to experience the totality of what we as humans have done to creation so that we can feel the effects that our actions have on us, how they make us ill. Here again by finding the Goddess we can help to heal the nature/technology split in the world.

Connecting with nature can happen in various ways, such as going out into the wild, or simply by working in the garden, which is a microcosm of nature. If you allow the garden to be fairly natural, then you will see more of nature than if you rigorously tame it. If you do not have a garden, you could have a window box or an indoor garden. With this contact we can meditate on the nature of the changes that nature in all her forms goes through. This involves going to the same place regularly so that we can note and feel these changes.

It may be that the recent success of various published nature diaries has been brought about by the realization that people want this contact, but in a form of reference that we are now used to — the written word. Through reading it becomes easier and not so 'foreign' to go outside and get direct experience. It is through direct experience that we attain an inner understanding of what is happening outside and how it relates to our lives.

From this general contact with the changing seasons of the year we can move to the specific changes that occur with certain plants and animals, and learn how these animals can help us in our contact with nature and her mysteries. As we have seen in Chapter 3, the Goddess of Change is associated with certain animals and plants which form part of the mystery, as they do in the alchemical tradition. These different animals are viewed in the flask as each new stage of the work is completed. The Changing Goddess also has different animals to represent the different stages of her changes, including the feelings and passions that arise at these times. These are the energies that we can contact through her and they are also energies that we can transform should the need arise, for instance if they have turned negative.

THE ANIMALS OF THE GODDESS

The snake is an important animal of the Changing Goddess mysteries in that she is the Changing Goddess in animal form. The snake lives in the rocks or holes in the ground, and similarly in the body of the Goddess or the earth. She completely changes her skin every so often which is like a rebirth. She moves like the energy of the spinning in an undulating fashion. She sleeps in a coil like the energy at the base of our spines. Her venom both kills and heals. Like nearly all the Goddess's animals she is nearly extinct. She represents the dark mother and the menstruating woman, because like all representations of the Goddess she can kill. (Traditionally, menstruating women are seen as having this power.) It is her coils and her motion that set the motion of the heavens. The serpent of wisdom is often rainbow-coloured in mythology. The snake guards the Tree of Knowledge. There is a strong association of the snake with the uterus, especially in Egyptian mythology. Snakes are often associated with wells as their guardians. Snakes are a symbol that can be either good or bad.

It seems strange that the snake has now been left with the negative symbolism only, and we all fear them, whereas the ancient Priestesses befriended them. There are statues in Crete where the Priestesses are seen holding snakes in their hands, and in a museum there are pots for the snakes to drink milk from. In the spiritual realms the snake is transformed into the fabulous dragon and serpent. These creatures which inhabit the realms of all the elements can be seen as creatures that unify rather than divide. There is also the plumed winged serpent, which represents the energies of the lower realm uniting with the higher. The serpent of the union of the elements would be the Ouroboros: the snake which eats its own tail.

In Celtic mythology song-birds are the blackbirds of Rhiannon. They live in the branches of the Tree of Life and are often brilliantly coloured, i.e. they have a spectral reflection in direct light. They symbolize thoughts and are believed to be human souls. Like the snake, birds lay the cosmic egg from which creation springs. They are like the swallows messengers of the Goddess. The Goddess has her song-birds which carry her oracles and give their blessing. They sing at twilight, welcoming the dawn and the dark. Like the snake they are killed for game and kept in cages. They are now shot while migrating so no longer have a safe sanctuary.

Bats are associated with witches and darkness. They fly at night, so are feared as they see when we cannot. They also suck blood, which is the life-force in mammals, so they are seen as bringers of death and disease. They are much maligned, so have become very rare. Another bird of the Goddess that is associated with the night is the owl, the bird of Athena.

Other birds associated with the Goddess are swans. Like snakes, swans shed their feathers and also change their colour as they grow. The swan forms a relationship for life with its partner, and is often thought to be a transformed woman. Swans are very closely related in their shape and flight patterns to cranes, herons and storks, which are also birds of the Goddess.

It was unlucky and a crime to kill birds with white plumage such as swans. White is seen as sacred, whereas black is seen as evil.

It is interesting to note that swans are associated with crowns and golden chains, symbols often seen adorning the Goddess. These are the gifts of the other world, so swans are associated with travellers to other realms. Etain and other mythological women were turned into swans and cranes. The Goddess wearing a cloak of feathers is a common meditation symbol and fits in with the shamanic idea of animal transformation for journeying. Swans are also associated with the Fates. In Norse mythology one of the images of the Goddess of Fate is a swan, and there are also the Swan Maidens of the Norse tradition.

The crane, stork and heron all look very similar and mythologically are interchangeable. They are associated with birth, hence carry babies. They are also seen flying in the spring so are believed to give their augeries at the time of the rebirth of nature. The legend of the crane bag which contains the magical treasure of the Isles of Britain is very similar to the bag of Athena which contained the sacred disc on which were inscribed the sacred vowels.

The spider is the emblem of this book from which we derive the mysteries of spinning and weaving. Cirlot[3] begins his section on the spider by giving three distinct meanings: 1) creativity; 2) aggressiveness, an aspect that much attention is paid to by biologists, as the female eats the male after mating; 3) the way the web makes a perfect spiral going towards a central point. Cirlot describes the spider sitting at the centre of its web as like the centre of the world or creation. It is related to Maya, the eternal weaver of illusion. In its creative and destructive aspect, its endless weaving and destroying is like the ceaseless alternation of the forces on which the universe depends, or like the constant inhalation and exhalation of the breath.

The spider is an animal of the moon, because the waxing and the waning of the moon is like the weaving of its web. It has some of the worst associations of any of the Goddess's animals. Most of the spiders are harmless, yet these insects cause great fear, especially in children. Yet I can think of no reason other than that they have many legs. When I see the beauty of their webs, I cannot stop wondering why an insect that produces so much beauty also produces so much fear.

Frogs and toads are also animals of the Changing Goddess. There are many superstitions and so they are treated very badly. They go through a metamorphosis from egg to tadpole to frog or toad rather like the Changing Goddess. It would seem that all animals to do with change are associated with the process of life and death, but especially with birth. Symbolically these changes are like the changes that a woman goes through from childhood to adulthood. They also have the ability to live both in water and on the ground, so are travellers between the worlds. Frogs often appear just before rain, which brings changes to the earth as the plants suddenly grow. In the desert, rain brings about the most extraordinary changes: the sands suddenly become covered in green shoots and flowers. The behaviour of the frog appearing and disappearing with the weather is in tune with our own natures. Our creativity comes and goes like the weather.

Jung believed that the toad is the antithesis of the frog. Toads have beautiful patterning on their skin, although this can cause rashes in humans. However, if left alone in the garden, they eat pests. So they play a helpful role despite being feared. Like snakes, toads are becoming very rare. It would seem that we are trying to eradicate any animal that is poisonous. Toads do not kill but can give hallucinations. These states of altered consciousness can be used to give us insights into ourselves. They are similar to the states that shamans go into when they are journeying, and are often induced by hallucinogens of plant or animal origin.

Another animal that is associated with the Changing Goddess and has a wondrous metamorphosis is the butterfly. It comes out during the heat of the day, and is attracted by the colours of the flowers. It transforms itself from a caterpillar which eats the veil of the plants, into a chrysalis which is like a veil wrapped around itself forming a boundary while it goes through an inner change to be reborn as a butterfly, which is the veil of the earth in flight up to the steller realms. This transformation is like the transformation of the self that we all hope to attain. Butterflies are believed to be the soul waiting to be reborn. In Irish mythology Etain swallows a butterfly and becomes pregnant. She was also a swan, which is another story of the transformation that a Priestess would go through. The moth is like the butterfly but in the world of the dark. It moves toward the light, and symbolizes light in the darkness.

The caterpillar of the silk moth produces the cocoon from which silk thred comes, and often sacrifices its life to give us silk clothes. Caterpillars, like spiders, form silken threads so that they can move from one leaf to another. Here the patterns of the weaving comes in again. Caterpillars and butterflies form patterns that are a form of protection from predators, and give signals that they are looking for a mate. So patterns were originally a way to help propagate the species and this is part of the spinning spiral. The constant rebirth of the species is like the repeating of the pattern in the cloth. As each generation appears, a slightly new pattern forms and the process continues.

Bees are also associated with the spiral of the Changing Goddess. The bee transforms substances; it makes the pollen of flowers into honey or the nectar of the Goddess. In ancient Greece the Priestesses of the temple were called bees (Melissae). The wings of the bee are like veils — another animal association to the veil — the place of creation. When the bees swarm, it is like the formation of a veil around the tree so that a transformation can take place. Fontenrose[4] states that honey is the substance that the Priestesses eat to get manic inspiration. As honey had great value he suggests that it could be the treasure that the dragon or python of Delphi guards. The honeycombed caves of the inner mysteries were often believed to be underneath the temple. In the caves, as in the honey comb, mysteries were performed.

The making of honey is a very complicated, alchemical process. In British folk tradition bees are familiars that you can talk to and tell all the news to, keeping nature informed of the events in human life. After the bees have been told of a significant event in the lives of those that own them, they are supposed to hum — the sacred sound of life, the vibration that causes life and change. Bees are the animal alchemists of the world.

Next come the animals of the Goddess which produce milk, like the cow which produces the food for both new life and the dead. They represent the Goddess in her nurturing aspect as the mother of life. Their horns are connections to both the future and the past, like a tree with its branches. We can contact our ancestors with these horns.

The hedgehog is one of my totem animals, and one that I have been very fond of since childhood. Gimbutas[5] finds that the hedgehog has a strong connection with the uterus, because of its similar shape. Hedgehogs are animals of the night and so are associated with the moon and change. They have a similarity with the moon in that they can go from being crescent-shaped into balls. In British mythology the hedgehog is believed to be lucky, as it can roll itself into a ball and then collect the wealth of the forest on its spines, especially the oak apples, which have special significance because they produce a black dye. The spines of the hedgehog are like the rays of the sun or the moon, which can be woven into the body of the animal for rebirth to take place.

I have concentrated on the animals of the Goddess that transform or that I have an affinity with. There are many others associated both with Changing Woman and the Goddess. We all have our own favourites. The animals that I have known since my childhood are a kind of family totem. This is an important exercise that can give some powerful insights into the family's energies.

Making a totem pole

Making a totem pole is an intuitive exercise. Decide on seven animals that have a special meaning to you and put them in an order from one to seven. They can be connected to the sacred centres of the body. When you arrive at a final arrangement, make a drawing of the totem pole. When there are any problems within the family, meditate to find the animal that is weak, and with drumming and singing re-empower it. This works well with both illness and emotional problems. Working with these poles you can learn to contact your energy. If one of the centres of your body needs more energy, you can dance that animal to raise the energy level of that centre. These totem poles can also become like a magic wand. All the different animals of the pole can join together to empower and heal others.

The unicorn is a mythical beast which in mythology is masculine and the companion of the maiden aspect of the Goddess. Its spiral horn is like the energy of the totem pole. The energies of the spiral horn or the pole mix together to form the cone of healing. Unicorns are the companions of the maiden. However, reading between the lines of the stories about them, I tend to think of unicorns as beasts that turn up at the times of transformation. In stories they appear just before the princess is about to marry, for instance in the wedding tapestries of the Claude le Viste in the Musée de Cluny, Paris.

THE PLANTS OF THE GODDESS

In this section I will concentrate on the aspects of plants to do with transformation and change, and their connection to the Weaving Goddess. Plants, like animals, transform themselves. These changes occur at the times of the changes of the seasons. With plants, as with animals, these changes are part of the yearly cycle of the earth. It takes human beings a lifetime to complete one cycle. Plants and animals go through several of these cycles. Trees can live for hundreds of years and are the longest lasting plants, although several lichens also live for hundreds of years. Mythologically, the tree is the queen of these changes. She is reborn into the shell of last year's tree, whereas many plants are reborn into the seeds of the next generation.

It has been shown that plants can communicate and feel, not as we know it but in their own language. Some plants have existed for millions of years, like the horsetail. They are the basis of our medicines, and their healing properties are phenomenal. Plants provide us with food and the raw materials for clothes and houses. Trees provide shelter and inspiration.

Trees also provide the resins and gums that are the basic ingredients of incense, which is a transformation substance in that it transforms our state of consciousness. Plants provide the essential essences for perfume, which is closely related to incense. Essential oils are used for healing and for the body's general well-being. Certain scents stimulate the mind in different ways. They have three vibrations: heavy, medium and light. These correspond to the three worlds, and if you wish to get in touch with one of these worlds, perfumes can help you.[6] Light scents go with the golden realms, for example lemon and sage; medium ones go with the twilight world, for example geranium and pineal; heavy scents go with the dark realms, for example cedarwood and frankincense. The most beautiful of the flowers and scents is the rose, but unfortunately the perfume is very expensive to work with.

Many plants contain essential oils that are made in the heat of the sun. These oils can be extracted to produce pure oil or the plants can be burnt and the oils released into the atmosphere. If several plants and resins are mixed together, an incense is obtained which when burnt will release these oils into the atmosphere. When we breathe in these perfumes, they go directly to the pituitary gland in the brain. The stimulation causes a response: some oils can make us relaxed while others make us more energetic. Some oils cause small changes, while others and other combinations can put us into altered states of consciousness. It is from these states that we can travel to the other worlds or the other realms within this existence.

These perfumes often make us breathe deeper, which helps us to move to these deeper states of being. At this point we begin to tap into the vital energy of plants in order to transform ourselves. This is most obvious in the image of the transformation of the grape into wine. We use it as a spirit to cause drunkenness, but it can also be used to transform us into states of ecstasy. Wine was used in the rites of Bacchus and other Gods. This state of ecstasy is one of the prime reasons for doing rituals in that in this state we can feel ourselves as divine beings and see the world as we imagine the Goddess does.

This is the state of the daylight world when it is contacting the light within the darkness. It needs to be in this altered state in order to move into the realm of the opposite. Many of the mystery religions had a time before the main ceremony when this state was reached in order for the participants to be open to all the forces. When doing large group rituals in a residential setting, the evening before the ritual is a time of moving into this state. It is a period of letting go before the time of winding up to do the ritual.

Another transformation of plants is the changing of wheat, barley, oats, corn into the bread of the Goddess. For bread-making it is traditional to use meal or grain crops, although acorns and other nuts can be used. In religions throughout the world bread is believed to be the body of the Goddess; by eating her body you received her wisdom. It is the same with eating her sacred animals. That is why so many animals are taboo, because they were once in the realm of the Goddess. With the takeover of other religions, what was once sacred becomes a taboo.

Bread has never faced this problem as it is such a staple food in our diet. The leavening of bread is achieved with yeast, which is a microscopic plant, and a transformative agent. Cakes have been baked for the Goddess in all cultures. This is also part of her mystery in that they start as dry ingredients, are then mixed with water or milk, go into the oven, and come out transformed. The oven is like the transforming vessel of the womb of the Goddess. The making of bread is full of mysteries, such as the mystery of its rising. Also recipes can become family traditions passed down as dishes to be baked on special days. There are many fairy tales and nursery rhymes about the baking of cakes, such as 'Sing a Song of Sixpence'. Bannock breads are baked for the Imbolc festival in the spring, and cakes are baked for all the fire festivals in the Celtic calendar. In Greek mythology cakes are baked for Hecate and left on the crossroads.

The mysteries of the growing and the cutting of the corn are some of the strongest and best preserved in the world. This is the transformation of a plant from a golden grain into a golden stem which is then cut and transformed into the bread or the corn dolly image of the Goddess of life. The cycle of the corn is also the cycle of the Goddess.

The apple tree produces the fruits of immortality, or the fruits for the other world. The branches of the apple tree are the wands which take us into the realm of the fairies to meet the Goddess of the other world.

Other plants of the Weaving Woman are the flowers and plants that dye the fleece. This is a very alchemical process: the dye is extracted from the flower, and other chemicals are added to make the dye fast in the yarn. These are called mordants and are often of mineral origin. Dye can be obtained from roots, berries, bark, leaves, lichen, crottle and flowers. The colours obtained from these plants vary according to place, climate, and the minerals present in the water supply. Dye recipes were passed down within families and were rarely written down, and with the invention of synthetic dyes most of them have been lost. Most plant dyes give the colour that you would expect. It should be remembered that the amount of plant needed is equal to the amount of wool being dyed, so they use a lot of plant mineral. So don't use plants that are rare, especially lichen, which can take a lifetime to grow one inch. Basic plants are lichens, cudbear, orchil, and lady's bedstraw for red and pink dyes. Yellow can be obtained from birch leaves or dyer's camomile; green from fern leaves and reeds; blue and indigo from woad. I have also used plant dyes for dyeing sand to use in sand painting. In general the synthetic dyes are easier to use, but the colours are not as pleasing as those made from natural dyes.

To make the girdle of the Goddess I feel it is worth the work and the long walks to dye the strands from plant sources. If you use black, red and white, the only part you need to dye is the red, since black and white come from the natural colour of the fleece.

For red you can try using bramble berries. These need the mordants of alum and cream of tartar, which are added to the dye bath while the water is cold. The whole lot should be brought up to the simmer and simmered for about an hour, then rinsed in hot, salty water. Another source of red is the lichen that grows on limestone. This is a long and more complicated process, where the lichen is fermented in ammonia, water and oxygen in a warm atmosphere for about three weeks. Towards the end of the fermentation process chalk or lime is added to give it the consistency to make into balls. A tablespoon of vinegar before the dying begins is added to the dye bath. Although this process is very fiddly, it is also great fun. If it is done with a magical intent, the process of transformation that the plant and wool go through can be a process that we also go through.

This is a different form of the alchemical process in that what happens in the cauldron or the flask is also happening inside and around us. If we look out for this in our lives, we can see the particular process that we are going through all around us. This is what Jung called synchronicity. If done as a magical ritual, this form of change can be felt in the body and seen in the way one's life changes.

The lichen dye is called Ochrelechia Tartarea — white crottle or orchil in English. In a book by Fiona Macleod[7] there is a reference to a Weaving Goddess who sits in the earth and weaves life upwards and death downwards. There is an interesting connection in that the growth of orchil is rather like weaving, creeping very slowly across the rock. The dye from the lichen is also used in litmus paper, where it shows the acidity or alkalinity of a substance. This demonstrates the idea of balance, and the finding of balance is what weaving is all about: a balance of the warp and the weft tension, in order for the cloth to stay flat. Orchil has been an inspiration for this book since I read Fiona Macleod, who caught the idea of the Weaving Goddess being very ancient, indeed the first to be formed on earth.

This shows that the connection between the earth and the feminine is very, very old and it is that connection that we as women are trying to find again through trying to heal the split between ourselves and the earth.

When I started on the path to the Goddess the first group that I started was a herb group in which we studied herbs to try to find out for ourselves what their healing properties were. This group stimulated me to form a herb garden, which I still have. I still use knowledge gained in this group when I work with others. It was in this group that I furthered my knowledge about incenses and essential oils. It then went on to form itself into a ritual group in which we continued the study of herbs and combined this with study of the seasons.

A group of this kind is very easy to set up and get inspired by. Ours was started with a group of friends, and then we opened it up to others from the green circle. We started by studying herbs by making them into teas and then seeing how the discussion developed. After an hour or so, we would discuss what we thought the essence of the conversation had been. We then looked the herbs up in the book to see if the discussion had been related to the properties described. Nine times out of ten this was so. It became very inspiring as we found that we were consciously as a group tuning into the herb that we had taken. We then developed this process by working with these properties in a more formal way, and contacting the spirit of the herb. This was done at first by individual meditation on the herbs and then reporting the findings. We found that this was more difficult, but it did eventually give us rewards.

While in the process of this study we discovered the shamanistic techniques of contacting the spirits of plants. We also used this method. I met the spirits of several plants. They were all different, and they are now my helpers when I use these herbs.

When I want to find the spirit of datura, I became like a bat with large black wings and went down deep into the dark. In this dark place we all turned green, and gave out a glow; at the bottom was a nest of green eggs. At the time I understood this to be finding hidden things in the darkness. The herb made me feel like curling up into the foetal position, and it felt as though the spirit had flown with the bat rather than the whole being that had gone on the journey.

The spirit of the elderflower took me to a hot and humid place in the sun where the scent of the flowers was overpowering. There was a woman doing a sensual dance. I felt very light-headed, as though I was slightly drunk. I started to dance with the woman and my body moved, as did hers. As I moved, I began to feel lighter and lighter as if things were falling away from me, which they eventually did as I fell into a sleep.

Orange blossom gives me the feeling of being by the sea in the sun. It reminded me of when I was in Malta. I feel like I'm being massaged and that I am becoming more and more relaxed. I feel arms or wings around me. I can see all the energy centres of my body moving together in harmony. My whole body feels very warm. I am lying flat out like at the beach.

These are lines that come from the journal that I wrote at the time, about seven years ago. I have been back to these places many times to get more information and to establish the contact. In the meditations that I did to find the spirit of the plants, I first noticed that certain herbs make me go into different positions.

We all journey in different ways. These journeys were done by having a small part of the herb in the mouth and then going in trust with what was happening in the imagination. Plant journeys frequently start with my feeling dizzy or spiralling down into another image. I now know this to be the start of a journey or trance. Later I learnt that others worked in this way as well. Anthropologists describe shamans taking days over these journeys and I am sure that to do it this way would make the journey stronger and more in harmony with the vision within the self, the environment and the world.

Having said this, a seven-day ritual is stronger than a 24-hour ritual. For me on these occasions the intensity of what happens is so strong that they become truly unforgettable experiences, and have a life-changing result. It is all about going with the flow of the moment or the ritual circumstances, which is how the plants and the trees grow. They develop according to the weather conditions, in harmony with this process.

Trees are the living representation of what we are doing to the earth, but we should not forget that the seemingly dead objects of the earth are also alive. From the rocks and the stones we can often see life emerging. They are alive, but on a time-scale so different to ours that they seem as though they never change. These stones were once hillsides, then they became rocks, and eventually stones, with the heat radiation of the earth. Some reached the sea where the stones eventually became sand. This takes millions of years — not days or months, which are the time-scales that we are used to.

The Changing Goddess is very much about time and the cycles of time. Part of her mystery is to connect with time-scales of millions of years, as well as the shorter ones. The boat of Isis is the ship of millions of years. It is the ship of the sun, which travels its journey every day, and has been doing so for millions of years. To re-establish our contact with the earth we have to make contact with this cycle as well. It is here that I feel we have a key to understanding our relationship to the earth. She is millions of years old, and it is with this cycle that we can find a place for ourselves, as we have the newest cells that she has grown. In our cells, our bodies we can find the newest energy of creation. We can feel her energy rising and falling, as we are still feeding from her breast. Unlike children, we never leave her breast. We have to find how we can give her back the love that a child gives to its mother. To do this I feel that we have to put a lot of the ideas that we have as a society on the compost heap and leave them for dead. Like the boat of millions of years we have to travel to the darkness. We have to move to the realms of the dead.

This is the chapter of the woman of the woods or of the desert, and it is in these places that we have to go to die and be reborn. She is the Goddess of the darkness that is behind the veil. It is in this place that things can be broken down in order for them to heal and reform. In the world we are all beginning to feel the need for this healing to take place. More and more people are looking for ways that this can come about. Some are working with the earth directly in planting trees and clearing up pollution. Others are campaigning politically. Many women are beginning with themselves as the start of this process, and turning to various women's groups to try to understand themselves and the world.

Recently, there has been a great resurgence of women's spirituality groups and women's groups working directly with the environment. The women at Greenham Common are an example of women's political action mixed with spiritual concerns. There are also more women entering therapy and taking the journey into the darkness so that they can die to be reborn.

S. Griffin's book *Woman and Nature: The Roaring Inside Her*[8] describes this process. We have something that is screaming inside ourselves to come out and be healed; to be heard; to be united with the outside. Until this voice is heard, the process of change will be very vague. The formation of the process cannot happen until we have heard all the sides of the story. Mary Daly uses the words 'helix' and 'spiral being' to describe the inner ear and its relation to women's hearing. The journey into the centre of our being is to hear this voice, to hear the voice of the earth so that we can work together for the good of both. We need this inner dialogue so that we can find what the inner part of our being needs, at this time. The book title *Freeing the Feminine* has been going around in my mind. This is the inner feminine voice that we need to be free and to be heard. It has been trapped within for too long.

The idea of giving the earth a voice has been taken up by the deep-ecologists. In the book *Thinking Like a Mountain: Towards a Council of All Beings*[9] the authors describe a workshop where the participants become part of the earth and speak for that part or for that being.

More thinking like this is needed so that we hear the voice of the earth once more. There is only one world. The other worlds of the light, twilight and dark are part of this world; they are not separate from it. The goals of humanity are freedom and development. I think this will come from our own individual creativity. We need to make all life sacred again. Living on the planet can have a sacred day-to-day reality. Spontaneity and planning can go together.[10]

As women we need to look closely at the connection between the domination of our bodies and the domination of nature. As individuals we are constantly trying to change the size and shape of our bodies. We also remove what nature put there, for example 'excess' hair. Is this not what we are doing to nature and the planet? The domination of nature is the domination of ourselves. For nature to be free we must be free. This freedom comes from within and without, and it is this that we should be working towards.

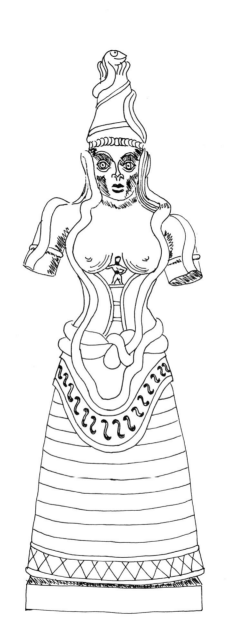

THE RED MYSTERIES OF MENSTRUATION

Menstruation is the great mystery of the Goddess, which this society hides. In 1987 I co-organised a conference on menstruation. I was surprised by women's reactions to this; some thought it was a very good idea, while others felt that menstruation was a private thing and they did not want to discuss it in public, let alone celebrate with others. I had always felt that because it was hidden we lost a lot of the sharing of a deep common experience. It was a mystery because it had been hidden for so long, and no one ever talked about it or only in negative terms. This, to me, was a waste of some very precious energy that could be used for the good of all rather than for the suppression of women. (At the time there had been some articles in the press in which women were portrayed as emotional because they suffered from PMT and did uncharacteristic things at this time of their cycle.) The conference was for the celebration of the mystery with others.

At the start of this conference we asked all the women present to draw their wombs, and put all the pictures on the wall. The energy that it released for everyone was amazing. It confirmed for me that for some women this was an area of their lives that have never had any form of expression. It is an important area that is often ignored or swept under the carpet in the hope that it will go away — which it does for three weeks every month.

To me, the most important book that was ever written for women is *The Wise Womb* by Shuttle and Redgrove.[1] This confirmed the hidden feeling that I had had for several years that because women menstruated they were considered unreliable by society. In Asphodel's article in *Menstrual Taboo*, red is the colour of life.[2] An inquiry into the taboos surrounding women's cycle by Asphodel gives the history of menstruation and the political consequences for women's lives.

Women's mysteries are often difficult to access in that they require a stillness of being that we do not normally have in this society. I rarely have the time to allow these deeper mysteries to come to the front of my thinking. It takes time and energy to bring these things up from the depths where I had hidden them. I wonder if I had hidden them because of the secrecy surrounding menstruation or because I often suffer from menstrual pain while I am bleeding. I also suffer from depression at these times and feel at my lowest rather than in the state of deep meditation that can happen in the later stages of bleeding. It is as if I have to work through some anger that another month has gone by before I can get into the mystery of the depths that this time can bring. At this time I can float endlessly in the depths of what feels like nothingness.

It was towards the end of one of these cycles that I discovered that if one found a place, the void, then one could find within the light of the being that is inside oneself. It felt like finding the door into the paradise garden, the garden of light that is within the garden of the darkness of the void.

It looks like the garden of the mysteries of the alchemist, full of roses and other sweet-smelling plants and trees. In the garden are the animals of the Goddess, and she herself is often there standing beside the well or the fountain in the centre. Gardens are a very important symbol of the mysteries in that they bring together the human and plants worlds with the spiritual. They are places of great peace and inspiration for me. The Hanging Gardens of Babylon were one of the seven wonders of the world, and the old gardens that I have visited have often had a spiritual dimension.

A garden meditation

Walk along a path until you come to a wall. Follow the wall along until you find a door in it. Find the key that will open the door. Go in through the door and find yourself in lush undergrowth. Follow the path through. Become aware of the animals and the birds making sounds in the garden. They are celebrating your entry into the garden. They are telling the others on the far side of the garden about your entry. Walk on through the undergrowth until you come to the inner garden. This is the garden of herbs and flowers. The garden is laid out like a labyrinth, and you follow the path around the garden and look at the flowers laid out in the beds and see how the colours change as you get closer to the centre. When you arrive at the centre you see a marvellous fountain with the sun shining through the droplets. In each droplet is a tiny rainbow. As you watch, the droplets start to form themselves into a woman, The Goddess of the garden appears before you and speaks. After your conversation with her you retrace your steps back to the gate.

Garden meditation in the garden of the stars

You walk across the rainbow bridge of the stars and go into the castle of the stars. Inside this white, shining castle is the doorway into the garden of darkness. In the side of the door is a handle which silently turns. You walk into the garden. It is so still and silent that you feel your breathing making sounds. Yet you know that this place is alive. You can feel this life as you breathe in; it flows into your body and all through your being. You become still, as the garden becomes still. You walk to the centre of the garden and look at the flowers. They are like tiny white stars on the ends of dark tendrils. The whole garden is white yet dark, full of dark, musky smells.

You go to the centre and sit on the chair in the middle. As you relax into the chair, you feel the scents of the garden beginning to overpower you. As you breathe in the fragrance, you feel yourself relaxing and becoming very still. The garden begins to spin, and the chair also spins. You feel your self moving down into another space. The spinning stops and you are in the garden again, but it is different. The stillness and the life that you felt before are still there but moving; you can feel the motion in the stillness. You can feel the earth and the plants moving and growing. You are at one with the breath of the garden and as you breathe with it you feel yourself becoming part of the garden. You become like the living beings in the garden. You feel part of this garden and the life within it. You sit and breathe so that you can feel your part in this garden and this mystery.

This is the outer garden of the stars, and also the inner garden of the mystery. As you sit in this dark and white garden, you become conscious of a red flower opening beside you. This is the ultimate mystery, and you watch it unfold as the light begins to change. The dew forms on the petals of the flower. Within this dew you can see a face reflected, and you and the face look at each other. While looking into each other's eyes you converse in

111

the deeper parts of your being. When the inner conversation has finished, retrace your steps back to the beginning of the journey. The light in the darkness in these mysteries is the light of the moon. The garden of paradise is the garden of the moon. After all, it is in the moon's light that plants grow. The light of the moon is very much part of the mysteries of menstruation, as are its phases. The light of the moon is a reflection of the light of the sun. It is often seen as inferior, since it is reflected rather than direct light, but the reflection is the mystery. In images of the Goddess, she is often holding a round mirror like the moon. In my meditation I often find myself looking at the reflection of the moon in a pool at the start of the journey down into the deeper and the outer realms.

It is the moon that is the inspiration for the Fates, and in the story of the moonspinners it is her light that they spin down into the sea. In Mary Stewart's book *The Moonspinners*[3] she retells an old legend that the moonspinners are naiads, and you meet them walking along the paths at night. Their task is to see that the earth gets its hours of darkness. They do this by spinning the moon out of the sky and onto their spindles. When the earth is in darkness the animals that are hunted at night can come out. The maidens go to the sea and wash their wool. As it floats up to the surface, the wool is wound onto the ball of the moon, and the light returns.

This is a good example of how the changes of the moon are connected to the earth and to the changes that happen to women during the different phases of the month. In the myth there is an underlying theme that there is a reason for everything including why the moon needs to change. It may be that having a reason for why things change makes it less frightening. Also the changes are part of the passing of time, and as each new or full moon arrives, oen has an idea of the passing of time. To the ancients the moon was the first clock. The moon is the primary symbol of the weaving mysteries; it is her changes that are reflected in the aspects. The new moon is the spinning of the moon, the full the weaving, and the waxing the cutting, while the dark moon is the time of rest before the new cycle starts again.

The phases of the moon also reflect the phases of the menstrual cycle. Opinions differ as to whether the menstruation phase corresponds to the new or the dark moon. I prefer the dark moon phase as the menstruating phase, in that at this time I am generally very tired and need a lot of sleep. So it fits in with my idea of resting at this time. However, my cycle does not fit in with the moon phases and I go from menstruating at the full moon to menstruating at the dark, with the flow most often happening at the quarter phases of the moon.

Although I keep records of my periods, I find that what has been happening in my life that month is more important than the actual moon phases in influencing my reactions at this time. I am very aware of the full moons and of feeling very different at these times. I also know that at the ovulation phase of my cycle I am very creative, whereas just after my period I become very organized, although it often does not last for long and needs to be sorted out again at the next new phase of my cycle. At times I feel frustrated that we have a calendar that is made up of weeks that relate to the moon but months that are not connected. I wonder how much more successful we would be as women if a month was a lunar cycle rather than a division of a solar cycle.

This inner cycle is the ruler of my life, and by working with it constantly I have a very clear idea of what I am feeling at any one time and how this relates to my body cycles. These ideas also fit in with the ideas of Dolores Ashcroft-Nowicki. She sees the womb as the sacred centre of the woman. It is to this centre that we can look when we want to find the sacredness of our being and the inspiration for our lives. Why, then, is the mystery of this centre never talked about? Why is it the most abused place of a womans body? Asphodel discussed in her article how what is now taboo or dirty was once sacred.

This was the inspiration behind the menstruation conference: to make menstruation a sacred activity again, which we could celebrate, in whatever way we wanted or felt was appropriate at the time. We made the conference 'women only' as we felt at the time that we had much to learn from other women about menstruation but needed the time to discuss this among ourselves, without trying to help men change their consciousness. I now wonder if I organized a conference like this again whether I would do it in the same way. I now feel that part of why the womb has become abused is men's ignorance of what they do not understand, so this mystery should be shared by men so that they too can learn how sacred this part of women's bodies is and help to regain its true nature again as a source of life and creativity for all. I imagine that this process involves women also learning about the sacred mysteries of the phallus.

I was very pleased to see in the new edition of Dolores Ashcroft-Nowicki's book that she had included a chapter on 'the ritual of reconsecration of the womb'.[4] This is a much needed ceremony and one which again affirms the need for women to make their wombs sacred again after abuse. This abuse can come in any form, even from ourselves, if we curse every time our period comes again. For some this abuse has been much worse, and the pain has been inflicted on them by others.

When I have performed this ceremony for others, I have been surprised at how powerful it is for all, and how brave some women have been in going through the ceremony. While doing the ritual I have felt some of their tension lifting as the ceremony has progressed. These rituals are extremely powerful in that they engage all the emotions and energies of magic at a very deep level. At the end I felt very connected to these women in that we had all witnessed the making sacred of our wombs and bodies. As I have participated in more of these ceremonies I have felt the healing of a small part of the womb of the earth that has been poisoned. This is the work that I feel Priestesses should be doing at this time.

Here we have the coming together of the mysteries of the earth and the mysteries of women in one ceremony. This type of ritual is the most healing, as it heals on a personal level and it connects us to the earth. It also heals on a global level as the ritual is usually done in groups. This work is the healing of the earth through the healing of ourselves. When I read books like *The Poisoned Womb* by John Elkington[5] I feel that we are in danger of not being able to heal the harm that has gone before. However, I do not allow this fear to dominate, as the work that is done now can only help.

These rituals are also very important in that the way that our wombs have been abused is very much part of the suffering that women are feeling at this time. In my work I hear stories of what women have been through in order not to become pregnant, or to heal themselves from the effects of contraception, or from the pain that has been inflicted on them by men in the pursuit of sex. Women who have survived these abuses are wounded. It is like the wound of the fisher king, which never heals.

Rituals like the one written by Dolores Ashcroft-Nowicki are a much needed start to the process of making the womb, once again, the sacred centre of our bodies. Perhaps if more women find this sacred place within themselves, we will begin to find the earth a sacred place once again. I hope that by women finding their sacred centres, they will be able to find the sacred centres of the local countryside. These wild places are still there, although as we turn the countryside into parks and put the old sites behind wire fences, as at Silbury Hill, they are becoming harder and harder to find. Perhaps part of the task is to stop the disappearance of the wild places so that we can reconnect with the Goddess in all her aspects.

It struck me very strongly when I was on the north Devon coast, with the wind blowing and the rain falling, how different the weather was here from in the city. In the countryside these storms have an almost magical feel where as in the city they are a nuisance. In the countryside the power of the elements is overwhelming, but perhaps have to be strong so that I could feel them. After having been in the city for so long I had become immune to nature and needed that strength to make contact again.

SACRED FLUID OF THE GODDESS

Blood was the sacred fluid of the ancients, although we see it rather like water, as something that can be replaced. Here is another example of how we have changed our attitudes towards things that were once sacred. This is the fluid from which life comes and without which we die. When we are born we are covered with fluid; it has a strong smell and a particular taste. Yet we seem to be frightened of seeing it. If we cut ourselves or see blood we go into a panic because we are losing some of our sacred fluid. It is the fluid of the cup of the Fairy Queen, which you have to drink in order to go to Fairyland. See the story of Thomas the Rhymer.[6] In *The Female Eunuch* Gemaine Greer suggests that we taste our menstrual blood.[7] I have had discussions in women's groups about this, and how some women felt that this blood was dirty and unclean. Others felt OK about the idea, but having tasted it did not know how to develop it. It was as though this was the first stage. We seem to have lost some sacred mystery that we can no longer access. I believe that the blood that was used by the ancients was originally the menstrual blood that can be obtained without sacrifice. It was this blood that was offered up to the Goddess: the sacred fluid that comes as the moon changes its phase, that is full of the minerals that can help the plants to grow.

Blood is the great mystery of the Goddess. It is probably what was in the cup offered up at her ceremonies of old. In the mysteries of the Grail it is what was in the cup, and in the cup of the Queen of Fairyland. It is to the altar of the Goddess that this cup is presented. The altar is usually a table on which a cloth is placed, like the veil of the Weaving Goddess. With this cup of our menstrual blood we present our inner self to the Goddess so that we can communicate with the inner Goddess who is behind the veil. We present to this altar the bread and wine that we have made from the body of the Goddess or the earth. At the time of the offering of our blood to the altar of the Goddess, we see the holy mystery unveiled. We have brought the moon down into our bodies, and the holy substance of life is revealing itself. If the ceremony takes place at the time of the dark moon we have brought the light of the moon into the time of darkness. She has appeared as light in the time of darkness. There may be a connection here between the Wiccan ceremony of the drawing down of the moon, which is performed at the full moon, and the appearance of the blood at the dark of the moon. In this ceremony the priest brings down the power of the moon into the priestess, and she is then connected to the power of the moon and the planetary forces.

The stone of the alchemists is the brown stone that bleeds, which is the same symbolism: the formation of a substance that bleeds and brings healing. This mystery may have originated in the mystery of the Cauldron of Cerridwen. From her cauldron come the drops of inspiration that can give a person the knowledge of life and death, as the cauldron contains within it both deathly poison and the drops of inspiration.

It is at the time of menstruation that the veil is thinnest and we can be most in touch with our inner self. This is the time when we can have the inner visions that can give direction to our lives. It is the time to go consciously into the great depths and find what is there. When we have gone through the darkness, we can find the light of the moon or the light that can illuminate our visions with the monthly flow of the blood. It is the time when we can go into the cave and shed our skins, like the snake, and come out refreshed and renewed.

In *The Wise Wound* the authors state that 'The Great Goddess's name in most cultures, in derivation means womb or vulva: the Great Goddess is creatrix. The womb gives birth and it also menstruates.[8] They also say that the way of all women is the menstrual rhythm; it is by these rhythms that we can live our lives. They suggest that the temples of the Great Mother were the colleges of women, where they went to learn these mysteries. I feel that it would be a good idea to set these colleges up again so that women can rediscover these mysteries. These are the divine laws of the Goddess, which she as Astraea came to teach us, and which we have forgotten. Within these mysteries is the knowledge of diet; certain foods can give us menstrual tension.

It also continues the knowledge of natural contraception and natural childbirth. In the literature on natural contraception[9] the changes in the cycle are shown by both emotional and physiological changes. The secretions are different at different times, telling us when we are fertile and when we are not. Our lives at present do not allow us this very subtle knowledge. There are too many things that can upset this delicate balance for it to be reliable, although many women do use this method.

The Wise Wound describes the sacred knot the Goddess, which tied the belt of the menstrual towel, and caught the magical blood of menstruation. Here again is the weaving mystery of the knot and the belt of the goddess. The belt would have been considered a sacred garment because it caught the blood of life. This is the substance that is life in our bodies and surrounds us at birth. In many ancient burials the bodies were covered with red ochre, possibly to symbolize that the body had gone for rebirth in the next world.

THE SACRED SUBSTANCE OF THE WEAVER GODDESS

The sacred substance of the Changing and Weaving Goddess is blood, which marks the changes of the month and of life for a woman. She goes from being a maiden who does not produce blood, to a woman who does, to a wise woman who no longer produces blood as she has the wisdom of the Goddess within her. Blood is the connection between the light and the dark worlds. When we are bleeding we are in the dark and ovulation is the light. The menopause is when the light of the Goddess enters the dark of the body, it also connects us to our ancestors.

This is the blood-link to previous generations and the knowledge that is contained within that line. We can connect with the ancestors by journeying, or through the horns of the Goddess, the tines being the branches of the previous generations. This connection can be made through meditation and through the sacred chanting of the names of our known foremothers. Connection with the ancestors at the present time is very important as we have to heal the wounds of our past mistakes so that we can move into the next age without the problems created by past generations. This is especially so in the area of the environment.

Blood is the connection between the light and the dark, the spirit and water of life mixed with the fire of the sun. It carries the soul, as it is the mixture of the feminine and the masculine. It is the seed of life.

6

WORKING WITH THE
MYSTERIES OF THE GOD

For women, working with the god brings up our deepest feelings about how we relate to both the Gods and the Goddesses. We need to look at both relationships so that they can be creative in our lives. For instance in my relationship with the dark Goddess, do I see all women in this manner? Do I look at men as I look at the Gods?

Do we have an inner man within us? If so, how does this inner man work and control our lives? Do we allow him to take control in the space between the worlds, the part of ourselves that needs to organize the intuitive material? We can find what we need from within, but we need to be able to organize this and put it to work, in our outer life, otherwise these ideas are a waste of our creative energies.

The outer man is the finished product, visible to the world. The inner man as the weaver wants to create himself. It is he who gets cross when he sees his ideas used by others and then getting the credit for what the deep inner woman has dreamed up. This is the relationship that my inner man has with my inner woman. The God has become old because his wisdom has not been used. He has the wisdom of the outer world and knows how these things can be used to the fullest in this world.

The relationship to the God is the polar balance to the Goddess. As I get more involved in her intuitive world I have made the pole of this balance even stronger. So the wisdom of this world seems even further and further away.

The Fates or Weavers are the Goddesses who try to keep these male parts up to the standards of the deep feminine. They give the male his challenges; they have a fighting nature. They are also the supporters, the nurtures and protectors. Following the path of the Goddess means knowing when to challenge and when to support; without both nothing grows.

We need to be able to stop the male from invading our being; to protect and support the self so that it can feel safe. Looking at several strands of weaving at once, we go across and then we come back again so the weaving can take place on a firm foundation, which gives safety for these ideas to be spread among all parts of the self rather than being jealously guarded by one part of the self.

In the creation myths it is the Goddess that creates the male principle in herself. I have to remember this so that I can create something that is of use in the world and that I can trust will work well. By refining the self I can refine the original of the male principle and form it into something that works for my good rather than bringing up the negative from the darkness of the unconscious. One has to change from feeding it cigarettes and sweets into feeding it things with which it can form a lasting relationship. We have to allow it to grow up and do our business, which is the joining of the conscious to the unconscious.

I feel that the answer to having a creative relationship with both the inner and the outer male is having a creative relationship to the self. To do this we have to understand our own boundaries. By keeping and acknowledging these boundaries we can have a full and creative life.

MY RELATIONSHIP TO THE MASCULINE

I have found this relationship to be a constant struggle which I have never really got right. I have got into my own creativity, but the formation of the work has been very hard. I often feel that I can do a task, but when I try to explain this I find that the expression of my understanding is not understood by others. I find this particularly with working with figures in authority. This is why I have associated this with the God and male figures in my life. I have the holistic, feminine understanding of life, but to translate this understanding to others requires the masculine approach and mode of expression.

How can I and the Weaving Goddess relate to this process? This is a project that I have been working on more, recently, but it is in its initial stages rather than a formed and finished idea. If the feminine mysteries in their essential form are concerned with the birth and the power of self-creation, then the male principle is the power to form and communicate these ideas in a way that does not diminish the feminine input but enhances the process.

I have looked at Jungian ideas such as the animus or the inner masculine within the woman, which I have found a useful model to start my explorations. It is the idea that within the outer feminine is an inner masculine, with which we have to form a relationship. I feel that it is important here to distinguish here between what I see as an inner masculine and the male society in which we live. The inner male is not part of the archetype of the male that is portrayed in the media but an other with which we want, or already have, a relationship. It is other to us in the sense that it is something that feels strange to our true being.

I first became aware of this inner man in my dreams. It came into my dreams at the time of ovulation and was often in the image of a dark figure that climbed through the window into my bedroom at night. At other times it was a man dressed in black who would ride away into the distance. I had the feeling that he was far away, a person to whom I would like to talk but who was very aloof. He rarely stayed long enough for any conversation to take place. I have also in dreams been to his funeral on more than one occasion. In other dreams the man has been older and with this man I have had conversations, although I tend not to give him the trust that he is requesting. In Jungian terms, I have thought of this man as my animus. It would appear that he is someone with whom I do not have a very good relationship. He could also be what is called the demon lover of the menstrual cycle who, in the mythology of old, is the conceiver of children. Other than this, I had no idea who or what he could be, or of what use, if any, having a better dream relationship with this person would be.

Magically, rituals involving the God have not formed a major part of my work. I have been part of a ritual to Dionysus, which was a ritual act of worship to the god, and several rituals which used the characters of the Arthurian legends as their main inspiration, including the figure of Merlin. Here I have found myself in the role of Morgan and in a very destructive rather than a creative and supportive mode. This has not surprised me because I feel that the Arthurian sagas are full of anger against women.

In rituals within the Celtic pantheon there are some very strange men to whom I have been strongly drawn. The most powerful of these is the Lord of the Faery, Midir. I felt I was being drawn into a world where I could drown in the scents that it evoked. Here dwelt the demon lover, a character that I would do anything for and would follow anywhere because of the feelings of love that he inspired in me. Another character with whom I could have had a good relationship was the God of the sea, Mannanon. He is very like Merlin, but much more etheric in that he does not have so much of Merlin's earthly, scheming side. These are all rather unreal men in the sense that they are idealized, and they are not really the sort of men that one could have a real relationship with. They remind me of the characters in my dreams in that they are unattainable, and therefore safe.

These ideas initiated my exploration of the role of the God within the mysteries of the weaver. After all, men go through a series of changes similar to women. They change from boys to warriors to wise men or sages. So for men there must be a similar cycle to the one for women. Is this a cycle that runs parallel to the feminine, or is it one that crosses at various points? This would fit in with the ideas of the weaving. Where it made the cross would be the place of the crossing of their paths. This would support my ideas that there are both women's and men's mysteries, and there are mysteries that are for both. All need to be explored in the full understanding of the mysteries as a whole.

It may be that one of the crossing points of the mysteries is the decision whether or not to have children. This is a question that all women have to face at some time in our lives, which can be approached in several ways. We can make an intellectual decision about the matter; we can make an inner body decision; or we can decide using both.

In mythology there are many women who do not have children, the most famous of these being Queen Guinevere and Brigit. These women, however, are the guardians or midwives of others' children and so do have some contact with children. This decision affects women very strongly, especially if the decision has to be made in a hurry during an unplanned pregnancy. Here the decision is influenced by the emotions of the moment and it is very difficult to think clearly about long-term objectives without reference to this sudden change in one's inner being. This is the time to go into the inner void or behind the veil of the Goddess and decide what is the best course of action to take at that time, giving the situation two to three weeks to allow oneself to go through the full cycle of emotions. It is very important for a decision to be made before the time is up rather than after. This is very difficult, because if the decision is to go for an abortion, the urge is to get it over very quickly.

To help make the decision, I suggest that you take an inner journey to the centre of the spiral or the void. There you can encounter the inner teachers and guides who are able to give advice on what would be best at this time. In this place one can also contact an animal of power who can give advice. It is these inner decisions that have the strength to help you communicate to others what decision you have made. I think that these journeys or meditations are the best way for dealing with this sort of problem because they give direct access to one's inner feelings.

Abortion is still a very emotive subject in our society. This is very unfortunate, because I feel that it is very much a personal decision, and that women should be supported in whatever decision they choose to make. In the past different societies have had different attitudes to this, some for and others against. It would appear that in the past women used herbs to induce miscarriage. I must stress that nowadays we no longer have this sort of knowledge and so advise against this method as it could result in poisoning of the women rather than miscarriage. Emotions around this subject run so high that it is very difficult to give a reasoned argument any more, but this is where the meditations will help. If you know yourself well, you will be able to make the decision without causing inner or outer emotional problems.

Those that have gone through this experience and found that they still have anger or sadness attached to the decision might find that working with the cutting aspect of the Goddess would be of benefit. To cut off could release a lot of energy and allow one to move into the future rather than reflecting on the past. The ritual of reconsecration is also very helpful, because it re-establishes one's own sacredness after the invasion of the operation. In the adaptation of the ritual that we use, we have put in a part about regaining one's original virginity and one's birthright. The ritual also contains an optional part on forgiving men, which might help in releasing the energy that is tied up in the anger if this has occurred. In these cases we often blame a man to some extent for what happened and what we had to go through, which they did not. However, men often feel guilty, although this is rarely expressed to the woman concerned.

In addition to this outer man with whom many of us have a relationship, there is also an inner man. This is an idea of Jung's with which I do not wholeheartedly concur, although it is worth exploring. I feel that Jung works mainly with the masculine and the principle of Mercurius, and that the Divine Feminine does not get enough of a place in the process, although other Jungians have tried to work with this principle. However, what they say about the inner man does give us useful pointers to the way that we can work with the Weaving Goddess.

In Chapter 2 we looked at the different stages that we go through when working with and meeting the Goddess. In working with the inner masculine we can go through a similar series. These are very clearly layed out by the Neumann[1] in his theory of the psychological stages of the feminine. Briefly, the first stage is the relationship with the mother archetype and the world of women. This is the Great Mother archetype where we experience the mother as similar to ourselves. Because of this, our development as women is very much in relation to our mother, whereas men develop in opposition to the mother. Neumann says that it is possible to live in this state without moving on to any of the other stages, and this results in a woman being very female-orientated because she exists only for the so-called female options in life. She has children, but is interested only in them rather than in her relationship with their father. She stays within the circle of the female in the family and is very dominated by the mother and her wishes.

The next stage is experienced as an over powering intoxication in which the woman feels the God welling up within her. The Gods associated with this phase are Dionysus, Osiris and Shiva: Gods associated with orgiastic worship by the feminine. They can also be experienced as the rain, wind, as lightning and as golden light. It is in this form that the woman feels that the male has penetrated her. She is moved into an experience where she goes outside herself. The woman feels that she has to surrender to this force, and it can bring up fear. In some cases this can change the masculine into the dragon or monster. All these forces are, however, associated with both the light and the dark; they are myths of the man in the moon. In dreams, these men tend to visit us at the time of ovulation.

When talking of this phase, Neumann also says that the body and the mind both have to have this experience before total understanding is reached. The problem with this phase is that a woman can have a strong relationship to the spiritual father and become fixated with this image rather than moving to the next phase. She can also become the 'woman without a shadow who is unfruitful because she is cut off from her earthly shadow.'[2] In other words, she becomes totally associated with the light side of the feminine and cannot relate to the darker aspects such as her anger and destructiveness.

The next phase is an outer form of marriage. The change is into having a real relationship with a man, relating to the masculine both on the inner and on the outer. This sort of relationship is fraught with difficulties and can take up the main part of our lives if we are not careful. We have to relate to and trust a force outside ourselves, which can be very difficult in a patriarchal society where everything is against this sort of relationship working for a woman. Ann Ulanov in *The Feminine*[3] uses a marvellous quote from Jung to describe how to overcome this negativity that we find in society:

> Love, her most personal, most prized possession, could bring her into conflict with history. . .
>
> No sooner does she begin to deviate, however slightly, from a cultural trend that has dominated the past then she encounters the full weight of historical inertia, and this unexpected shock may injure her, perhaps fatally . . . if she submits to the law of love, she finds that she is not only in a highly disagreeable and dubious situation . . . but actually caught between two universal forces— historical inertia, and divine urge to create. . .
>
> No one can make history who is not willing to risk everything for it . . . to declare that her life is not a continuation of the past, but a new beginning.

Finding this sort of individuality is the struggle to find a real relationship with others. However, society does not foster this as it is a very individualistic approach that would require a society where we were seen as individual rather than part of a collective born in the imaginations of the politician.

I used to very much want a Hero to come and save me from the life that I was living. This did (in many ways) happen to me, but I was very surprised that it was not 'happy ever after' and that the saving was the start rather than the end of the problem. I found myself in a relationship where on the surface everything felt fine, but underneath the earth was erupting. I found it very difficult to live with this new relationship and discovered that it interfered with my life. I had to take another's wishes into account all the time, so no longer felt free. This was the greatest surprise of the relationship, the loss of freedom as the price of being saved. I felt very much like Psyche in that I had been saved and then I had to look at what I had been saved by — not a handsome prince, but in the dark an ugly monster. It took me years before I could really look at this monster and see it for what it was, rather than what I thought it was in my fantasy. I found this difference from the myths very frustrating. He did not turn into the prince as promised. It is in this phase that we have the opportunity to discover what our needs from others are and how we find others' demands on ourselves.

In the next phase, still in a relationship with another, we relate to the other from our own centres. The relationship consists of two individuals together working from their individual centres. This involves working with both the masculine and the feminine in each partner. It is to the partner's self that the other relates and with whom the relationship is formed. The true selves of each partner are shown to the other. It is the finding of and the ability to show this true self that is the process that occurs at this stage.

In Jungian literature there is much discussion of the animus or 'inner man' of a woman. In Ulanov's book there is a very interesting section where she discusses the ideas of Irene de Castillejo, who suggests that the animus is a torch with which we are able to see and understand more clearly, and how we use this is different in individual women. Castillejo describes the animus as 'an autotomous spirit whose sole role is shedding light, focused light, light for its own sake.'[4] This is like the sensation of being in the void of creation when we find the light of the darkness, which can help us to see. It has no emotional function; it is there for illumination, and what we do with this knowledge is up to us.[4]

These four stages that are outlined in Neumann and then developed by other authors are very similar to the four aspects of the Weaving Goddess that were described earlier.

The first stage is the Rainbow Woman, the spinner, who forms her life from what is around her. She is the one who looks at the history of the Goddess, who discovers the history of the feminine and the Great Mother and looks at this in relation to her own life. She finds the world of the mother both in the positive and in the negative and sees how she relates to this.

Having worked with this, she is free to find that which is other to her self and see if she can relate to this in any way. This is the next phase, the time of the Weaver or the Trickster Woman. She is the one who is venturing out into the unknown, the world outside herself. She looks at the world of the male and the masculine. In this phase some find the overpowering ecstasy of this world. This is the place of the Demon Lover, and of erotic love of another who exists in the imagination. Yet this image, which comes up from within feels real. We work to free ourselves of this, which feels good but somehow not quite real or satisfying enough.

We then move to the next phase, of real relationship, when we meet the wise woman in ourselves, which we can show to others.

We also relate to this part in others. This is a time when we explore the true self in ourselves and in others. We become in touch with the earth and her seasons; we also contact the stars and the realms of the infinite. Here we realize the limits of our knowledge, that life is full of new and infinite possibilities. In a sense we start the cycle again but this time from our own centre.

In this book I have talked of these phases moving sequentially. Unfortunately, they do not. My experience is that they are all happening at the same time; I can see parts of myself in all of these phases, which are not linear but spiralling. The different phases occur in all of our lives at different times. Here it is useful to have a cycle that uses all the aspects at once. Then we can try to find which aspect it is that we have become stuck in when things are not working as they should do. In the world of the present, things rarely go as we expect them to. So this way of working can be a help at these times.

WORKING WITH THE GODS

This is a difficult thing to discuss in the short space of this book, but it is an issue that is often missed in books dealing with the Goddess. The problem is that most of the Gods in some way represent a patriarchal take-over of the Goddess-based religion, and that they are usually the children of the Goddess. Yet in most creation myths the first thing that the Goddess creates after nature and the earth is a consort for herself. Whether she needs one or not is a different issue. In some cases she is an autotomous woman, in others she has a relationship with a male consort.

A question that I am frequently asked is: if the Goddess is supreme, what is the role of the male and of the God? I have no good answers to this question. However, men do represent 50 per cent of society, and if we wish to have good relationships we should try to understand some of the myths and legends of the God. These legends are often an attempt to understand the feminine. There is certainly more to men than the procreation of children. I suspect that they are there for us to relate to so that we have an external measure, not to measure ourselves against but as a challenging potential so that we do not stagnate.

In the 'green' movement these ways of thinking are coming together in local community initiatives and in holistic ways of thinking. This is a great step forward and will, I hope, eventually allow us to be centred in relationships between the sexes.

One way of understanding the male is through the God. In the

Grail legends, and other myths, the male has stolen the treasures of the Goddess, and in some cases it is the male in the form of the spiritual father that has these treasures in his keeping for humanity to use. However, if we think of the male in the role of animus or torch-bearer illuminating the inner darkness of the feminine, we can see that these treasures have been brought into the light for us to use.

The problem is separating men as individuals from the patriarchal society in which we live, and the external male Gods from the internal masculine that is a way of describing certain urges that we have within us. In some ways they are all the same, in others they are all different.

There are three main types of God. One is the wise God who in British mythology is portrayed as a Merlin figure. From his relationship with his sister we can learn about the male–female non-sexual relationship. Secondly, there is the consort of the Goddess or the lord of the Forest, for example Herne the Hunter. Thirdly, there is the God of ecstasy, who is most often described as Dionysus. All these Gods have something to teach women, and can help society to allow a space for the feminine rather that keeping it in its present prison.

LOVE OR FREEDOM?

This is the question that at some time we all have to face in order to find where our path is from here. We all want and need love, but we also want freedom so that we can continue with our task in this world. If we know or at least have some inkling as to what our path is, then it is to this question that we will have to address ourselves. Love connects us to another and to the wishes of both rather than ourselves alone. Men have an advantage over women here, because they have separated from their mother at an earlier age and so can use this separation when following their path or career. This is more difficult for women, because we do not make this clear separation, but we need to if we want to choose freedom over love, which binds and ties us to another. It is towards freedom that we have to move so that we can find freedom within to stay on our true path.

This is the realm of silence. In silence we can find this path, but we also need to be silent with others so that we can just be with them rather than continually talking and creating the new. In some old cultures babies are taught to be silent so they do not give away the place of the tribe. However, they are silenced not with harsh words but with loving embraces. As small children they learn to keep quiet and to address the world with vision rather than with voice. We have to find ourselves in the realms of silence so that we can be with others but still have the vision of the path that we are treading.

The loving embrace allows us to feel safe, but the vision is unhindered, so that it can follow its path and go to the places of inner wisdom that can bring us true meaning. We can survive in the world of others and in the world of aloneness, both bringing their own beauty. Being in this world of silence allows us to go on vision-journeys and to feel safe so that we can get the full value of what we are doing and be able to return to this world seeing with the silent vision of wisdom.

It is this type of vision that we need to enable us to see and make the choice between love and freedom. It is the splitting from the family to begin the journey that starts both within and without so that one can find both freedom and love of others that can be contained within that love. It is like wearing a veil and withdrawing to find this freedom.

When I left home, I started by finding myself in relation only to myself rather than to what I felt others wanted me to be. Eventually I realized that it was the inner self that would have to change rather than the outer. I had changed the outer self so often that no further refinement was possible without the inner self changing.

My own freedom came from no longer worrying about what the outer world was doing, but transferring my concern to what my inner world was about and how this related to the outer world. I then became interested in my own art work again after a break of eight years, and returned to some writing that I had done only under pressure previously. I now want to move on to dance and voice work, and to other creative media that I learned while very young were not within my own freedom.

Within this freedom it is possible to find love, but this love is a very different love from the kind that I found when I was looking for love and not for freedom. This sort of love comes only when you have found freedom and creativity. It is then possible to be with others without one's mind wandering all over the place. Time planning is invaluable in the quest for freedom. If you know that you are going to do a particular task at a particular time then you can let go of worrying about when that task is to be completed and get on with thinking and doing other things. This gives us the time to be with others and to live the communication side of our lives to the full.

There can be a problem in getting creative inspiration at the times when we have planned it into our week, especially when there are strong emotions around or we are tired; sometimes it is hard to get started. This is where ritual can be very useful: one can invent a starting ritual of one's own. This can either be done at the start of a new project or at the start of each working day. If you examine your day you will probably find that you already have several starting rituals — perhaps a cup of tea or a morning shower.

BOUNDARIES AND SPACE

These could be alternative words for freedom and love. Freedom is space, and boundaries represent love. Boundaries and space need to be properly maintained so they are not constantly infringed by society and others, otherwise we no longer know who we are. We become a mixture of what society wants and what we think that it wants, but very little of what we ourselves want to be. For example, we might become like a man rather than finding the inner feminine. Removing these outer layers becomes more like rape, than a voluntary peeling down to the core. We become very frightened that there will be nothing underneath. The self has retreated so far inside that it has almost disappeared.

Magic allows us to re-establish some of these boundaries. We can form for ourselves the space within the boundaries, so that we can recreate the self and our wants and needs within. This is like the egg at the centre of the mysteries. The egg has the boundaries that we need but it also has within it the space with which we can create the whole and changing self. It is also like the egg of the aura. We need to be working with it constantly and to be sure that it is not getting tangled up with others or with emotions that are not positive to our well-being. This is very difficult to do. Often we do not realize what is positive and what is negative in our lives at any one time, except in retrospect. It is more easily realized if we have our own space where we can go to find the true self, to bring it out and work with it at all times.

This is why meditation is so useful and powerful, as with it we can go to this space every day and remember who and what we are and what it is that we want to achieve with our lives. Here we can make any alterations that are necessary to our lives. This is how we create the path that we want to walk along: we change the stones of the path so that they contain what it is that we want in our lives. It is not the end of the path that is important but the path in itself. It is the way we live each day and the way that we feel within that day rather than the sum total of our whole lives that we need to be in touch with. However, it is this that we most often forget as we tend to live in yesterday or tomorrow, neither of which is of any help when we are working with the Weaving Goddess, since she changes throughout each day and each year. This is her cycle.

I like to work with the Goddess differently within each cycle. In the daily cycle I like to remember the inspiration of the night in my dreams or first thoughts of the day. I like to remember the events of the day in a meditation, and the Goddess in a remembrance of how she has influenced my life during that day. I keep both a dream diary and a diary of the events or thoughts of the day. These are not sacred or special, and I don't fill them in every day, but mainly when I want to review my feelings or thoughts. I rarely reread them, but keep them as a tribute to the changes that I have made so far. However, when I have reread them I have been shocked to find how many times I have gone around the same garden before moving on, and had to repeat the same lesson several times before finally learning what it was that I was doing and how to solve the problem.

I like to remember the Goddess or the deity that I am working with at the same time every day, as this is very much part of keeping in touch with the inner mysteries, even when I am very busy in the outer world.

I review my thoughts of one month at the times of the full and new moon. This can either be through doing a ritual to the moon or in a review of what I have done in the last month. While making this review I compare it with my menstrual chart. In *The Wise Wound*[5] there is a menstrual mandala, which is a very useful way of putting all these things together. (See Chapter 7 for some more ideas on this.)

For one year the review that I do is to reread what I have written during the year. At the beginning of the year I also like to make a list of things that I would like to achieve in this year. I see how many of these I have achieved and how close I have got to others. I then write a list for the coming year.

I have recently thought that it would be a good idea to do a similar review of what I would like to achieve during this lifetime.

ALTARS TO THE GODDESS

When I have sorted out these thoughts and ideas I give them to the Goddess and put them on her altar. This is like giving them to the void. The desire to find love in freedom was one of the things that I put on her altar. Throughout the house I have several altars, and it is to these that I go when I want to remember the mysteries and the Goddess. I sit before these alters when I want her help.

I have a main altar in the temple on which are the objects that I keep for the Weaving Goddess. In the bedroom I have an altar to the parts of the Goddess that are sacred to myself or the Goddess part of myself. It is to the things that resonate with me rather than to a particular diety. On this altar I have a disc that is one of the first ritual objects that I ever made. I have a series of globes of the planets, the sun and the moon; stones and other interesting natural objects that I have collected; various knitting needles, two very large shuttles, and lots of crystals. These objects vary as I move them around the house. I often wonder, as they move around the house, how their function in my life is changing.

I also have an altar to the God, which is very informal. It usually contains objects that I like, but associate with something other than myself. My favourite for this altar are poems by men.

Altars are like paintings for me in that they reflect the way I am at the time that I set them up. They are also about the issue of space and boundaries. The altar is the space that we can give to this side of our self but the edges of the altar are also the boundary. I feel that for me it is very important to give this space within the room. It is also important that it is within the context of my life and that my other interests also have a space within which I can express myself so that the spiritual side of my life does not take over, and leaves me room for my outer interests as well as the inner interests.

Working with altars to the Goddess can be very interesting as these can give much information about ourselves and the Goddess. They can be used in their entirety as a symbol for meditation, or each symbol can be used separately for meditation and then arranged so that both the part and the whole have a message.

Working with symbols is a very strong way of working with the Goddess energy. Most of her images come to me in the form of symbols. The principal symbols of the weaving aspect of the Goddess are the spindle, the loom, the shears and the veil. The

134

spindle symbolizes the magic wand of the feminine mysteries. It is also like the Tree of Life of the mysteries and the swinging pendulum of the dark and the light, and much else besides. The loom symbolizes the creation and the formation of the solid, making the pattern of time in the coming together of the dark and the light, the cross of balance and the connectiveness of the web. It is the mechanism from which life is formed. Its threads are the threads that connect us all together.

The shears are the instruments that cut us apart and remove what is no longer needed. They are the symbols of the completion of the process. This is the most misunderstood aspect of the Goddess in that it is here that we have the most fear and where we are likely to skip the process in order that we may go on to the new, which can seem shiny and bright in comparison. Endings are very important, and it is a good practice to get them right so that they can be used as a platform on which to build. It is very important to finish things fully, otherwise monsters from the past will come and hunt us out.

The veil is where we go to rest; we can go behind it to find another world. Behind the veil is the place where the wild woman lives; she is the part of ourselves that lives in freedom. When we acquire the veil or the mantle of the Goddess we will be free to find love. It is here that we will meet our true partner. This is the path of freedom to true love.

This is the magic of our everyday lives. Even if the magic has already happened, we still need to do the ceremony so that there are no loose ends left untied. After the cutting of the cloth comes the tying of the threads before the garment is finished. It is easy to forget that we have to contemplate the final article before we move on. We need to see what we have put into it and how we have changed as a result of the process. We can see the true beauty of what we have created, which does not shine as brightly as the new but still glows. We can often miss the glowing. With true reverence it can also shine like the new, because after all it is a new thing in its creation. It can be used as the start of a new process if we allow this to become the foundation for the next part of our journey.

This is the true way to work with the Goddess: we allow the old to be the foundation for the new. It is like waking up in the morning and working with the dream of the night during the day, and being led by our inner visions. We are present in our emotions when we do this; we are living in all the worlds at once rather than just in one world at a time. It is in this here-and-now time that we can find how the Goddess works in our lives. This is the time and the space that we move into when we are meditating and when we are doing rituals and ceremonies to the Goddess. It is here that we feel that time has a different quality: it either goes very fast or, more often, it stands still. This is the quality of being in the moment, which is out of time as we know it. Time, after all, is a constraint that is put on us by society and is arbitrary. We could have all sorts of other time systems such as lunar or stellar time rather than solar time.

When we have found ourselves we can work with the mystery of the other — the God. It is like going around the spiral again but on the other side.

7

THE ALCHEMICAL MYSTERIES

The goal of most magical work is to have a relationship with the woman of the other world. It is our movement in and out of her world that forms the basis of magical work and the work of the self. She is the higher self, the other-worldly teacher, and the companion on the path. She is the keeper of the doorway between the worlds and the resident within. Hers is the world where the colours are brightest, here we feel we are in the world of the young because time seems to go so slowly. Here we find a peace and vision that we can bring back into the world to help our own transformations so they can happen in another place and we can see this world differently.

To get into this world in a conscious way whenever we want to usually comes through the work: going through the elements and then through the levels of the worlds so that we eventually have a map and a pathway through. These maps are the best ways of working with magic, if we remember that they are maps and are not the real thing. They give us signposts and directions, but it is the landscape that we have to add. Each landscape is different, but most maps lead to the same place, another world where we meet with the higher forces that are the guiding and advising principles of the universe.

There are many maps around that are used for this process; the kabbala, the Tarot, and alchemy are some examples. All these give us systems for working with the powers of the universe in their many aspects. It can be very useful to make our own map of the universe and put onto this whatever we are working with at the time, then filling it out and extending it.

WORKING WITH MAPS

Drawing maps is a very good way of working with the changes that occur as we work with the Goddess. They can record the sort of experience that we have had or are seeking, which can be described as a mystical experience of the Goddess (Figure 8).

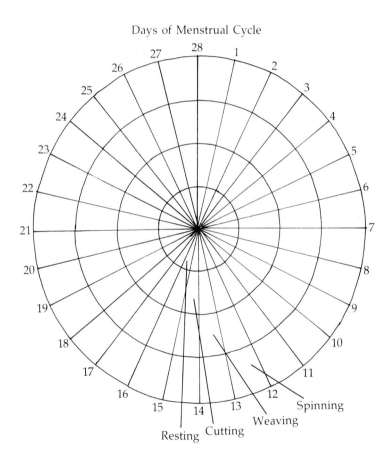

Figure 8 *The eye mandala can be used to write in feelings for each day in the appropriate section for the Goddess*

140

This is a feeling of being at one with the energies of the Goddess, the universe and the self all at once. It has the feeling of an orgasm of the spirit. One is left with a feeling of being in love with the world. These experiences come when we are least expecting them.

The first time I had one of these experiences was after a weekend workshop. At the workshop we had spent most of the workshop seated, and when I got home I felt like moving so I started dancing in my room. Before me came a vision of the Goddess surrounded by stars. When the vision left I was left with a feeling of great love. On another occasion in a ceremonial ritual I suddenly felt myself transported to another level, and for a few minutes had the feeling of being in contact with all the different worlds at once. I remember being very much in touch with the world that we call 'fairy'. The ritual was connected with this, and I had a view into these worlds very clearly. After all these experiences I have been left with the feeling of great love, which feels like the love of the universe and the energy contained within it. It feels unconditional, totally accepting, and very powerful. Afterwards one feels totally transformed through this experience of love. It is the sort of energy that fills up the inner being like a form of spiritual food. After this kind of experience I feel whole and complete.

Reading some of the writings of the female mystics, I found that they worked towards having this experience as part of their meditation practice. Teresa of Avila talks of having three kinds of mystical vision: corporeal, imaginary and intellectual. It should be remembered that both Teresa and Hadweijch (see below) were Christian nuns, and their visions should be seen in this context.

Corporeal visions are seen with the physical eyes; imaginary visions are seen with the inner eyes. Intellectual vision comes from a form of inspiration where there is no inner or outer form, just a feeling that something is there and communicating.

My vision of the Goddess surrounded by stars was a corporeal vision. My vision of the other worlds is imaginary vision, and the ideas that I have put into this book are intellectual. I use these kinds of ideas when I am working with clients in psychotherapy; often I am prompted to say something which seems disconnected to what is being discussed. Jung called this process transference in therapy; in magic it is a form of inner prompting.

This inner prompting is what causes us to change. It is the feeling of being guided that makes us try to find what it is that is prompting us, and try to envision it so that we can then move on to this next phase. This is why I feel that it is so important to envision what we want in our lives and what it is that we are working with. If we can see it, it can become real.

This brings us to a moral problem. Is it right to visualize what we want and to make it manifest? This is a question that we can each only answer for ourselves. I tend to believe that the things that we need will come to us, and the desires will wait until they become needs.

Hadewijch says at the end of her Vision of Reason: 'But love came and embraced me; and I came out of the spirit and remained lying until late in the day, inebriated with unspeakable wonders.'[1]

Teresa describes the feeling of her vision in a similar way:

> Often it comes like a strong, swift impulse, before your thought can forewarn you of it or you can do anything to help yourself; you see and feel this cloud, or this powerful eagle, rising and bearing up within it on its wings . . . . you are being carried away, you know not wither . . . the soul, when enraptured, is mistress of everything, and in a single hour, or in less, acquires such freedom that it cannot recognize itself. It sees clearly that this state is in no way due to itself, nor does it know who has given it so great a blessing, but it distinctly recognizes the very benefit which each of these raptures brings it. Nobody will believe this without having had experience of it. . .
>
> Ecstasy has the effect of leaving the will so completely absorbed and the understanding so completely transported — as long as a day, or even several days — that the soul seems incapable of grasping anything that does not awaken the will to love; to this it is fully awake, while asleep as regards all that concerns attachment to any creature.

These feelings remind me of the first magic ritual that I ever did. It was with the Green Circle in London and we had done a consecration in the element of earth. All the next day I felt a flow of radiance around me, and London seemed a very beautiful place full of interest. This feeling lasted for several days and contained within it a sense of being at home and having a place in the scheme of things for the first time. I also felt love for all beings. These feelings have returned from time to time. They have come back most recently when I have been working with the changes in alchemy. As I have worked through each of the changes and met with the alchemical Goddesses, I have found this state of being and this love at each stage of the process.

Hadewijch had the most amazing vision of what I would call the Alchemical Goddess, but to her they were the Lady Reason and her attendants:

> I saw in the spirit a queen come in, clad in a gold dress, and her dress was all full of eyes; and all the eyes were completely transparent, like fiery flames, and nevertheless like crystal. And the crown she wore on her head had as many crowns one above another as there were eyes in her dress . . . Before the queen walked three maidens. One had on a red cloak of state and carried two trumpets in her hands . . . The second maiden had on a green cloak of state and had two palm branches each sealed with a book. . . The third maiden had on a black cloak of state and in her hand something like a lantern full of days.

Hadewijch identifies the red attendant as holy fear. The attendant had said: 'Whoever does not hearken to my Lady will be eternally deaf to happiness and nevermore hear or see the highest melody and wonder of powerful love.' The green attendant is 'discernment between you and love. The black attandant is Wisdom as with the lantern the Lady sees the ''profundity of the depths, and the height of the highest ascent.'''[3]

The Lady is seen in a dress of all-seeing eyes with her aspects of Fear, Discernment and Wisdom. These are very like the alchemical Queens. In alchemy we have the Black, White and Red Queen as well as the Lady Iris who wears the dress of peacocks' tails. It is to these women that I look for change. They are like the aspects of the Weaving Goddess: they fit around the circle and give us different ways of looking at the processes of change that occur. If we add these women to the spinner, the weaver, the cutter and the resting/hidden woman, we end up with eight archetypes to work with. If we add the self we have the ninth.

The ninth can be seen as the Sleeping Venus that has to be awoken or as the spiritual principle that has to be brought down. The spiritual principle that I work with to bring things down is the Virgin of the Stars, Astraea. The underworld principle that I work with is the Venus of the Earth or the Queen of the Fairy realms. She could also be seen as Spider Woman — a power and wisdom of the earth that we bring up into consciousness.

The idea of the self as the ninth woman who is also the spiritual principle of the upper and lower worlds is very difficult to explain in words, and needs to be felt. The ninth is also the eye at the centre that can see through all the worlds. It is through this eye that we travel to the other worlds.

Going back to the Goddesses that I described in Chapter 1, they can be related to the nine as follows (Figure 9).

Spinner	Rainbow/Iris
Weaver	Athena
Cutter	Isis
Resting/hidden	Ariadne
White Queen	Maia
Black Queen	Arianrhod
Red Queen	Brigit
Peacock Queen	Nuit or Iris
Self	Faery Queen or Astraea

They are also related to the nine chapters of this book. The first four chapters relate to the Weaving Goddess. The White Queen relates to the chapter on male mysteries, the Black Queen to the mysteries of silence, the Red Queen the mysteries of menstruation, and the Peacock Queen to this chapter on the mysteries of alchemy. The self is the last chapter.

These nine women make up the circle of nine. They are the archetypes that are the guardians and the teachers of the universe. How we see these nine is very individual and a matter of personal taste; others have described them differently.

Caitlin Matthews in her book *Elements of the Goddess*[4] uses the names: the Energiser, the Measurer, the Protector, the Initiator, the Challenger, the Deliverer, the Weaver, the Preserver, the Empowerer. These nine make up the one Shaper of all.

Cherry Gilchrist in *The Circle of Nine* uses the names: the Queen of Beauty, the Weaving Mother, the Lady of Light, the Queen of the Night, the Great Mother, the Lady of the Hearth, the Queen of the Earth, the Just Mother, the Lady of the Dance.[5]

In Arthurian mythology there are the nine sisters of the Isles of Avalon, who include the Lady of the Lake and Morgan Le Fay. The nine-fold sisterhood of the cauldron of Cerridwen and the

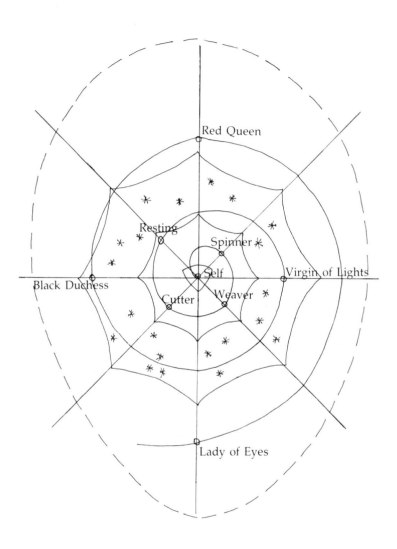

Figure 9 *The circle of nine*

nine muses are other examples. In Chapter 1 I used the stories of nine Goddesses to show the changes that we go through when we walk the spiral to the self and to transformation. These figures are similar to the Queens that I have mentioned as being part of my own circle of nine. These are the maps that I use to explain what it is that I am doing and how it all fits together. These women are the teachers that help us on the path, although they themselves subtly change as we work with them.

When I first started this work with the Goddess I began with the awakening Rainbow Woman who was the woman of the seven colours, symbolizing the awakening of the Goddess energy within. The cycle then moved to the emerging Trickster Woman, the clown or harlequin, who is the mirror of what we are doing, the tested, and the mask. It is her who takes off our masks so that we can see the real self. The cycle then turned to the journeying Dancing Woman, who has the knowledge and the wisdom to understand the visions and the dreams that we have and put them to use in the world. The next turn of the cycle was the spirit Wild Woman, the woman of creation and of power, a woman unto herself. She is the wise woman of the forest, often called the witch in the wood. She is the resting phase of the cycle where we go when we want to be alone with ourselves.

These four phases of the Goddess correspond to the phases of the moon: the waxing, waning, full and new moon. They are also the spinner, the weaver, the cutter and the hidden, resting aspect. I began with the idea of the moon and how this connected with the menstrual cycle. From working with this by recording my menstrual cycle on a moon calendar I began to find that my emotions were different at different times within this cycle. I began to give these emotions the image of a type of Goddess or female being; these then turned into the images outlined above. As I worked more with these images and started to do workshops using them, my ideas began to seem too complicated. I wanted a simpler way of explaining the Goddess, which people could relate to without difficulty.

I was reminded of the Goddess of the Spinning and Weaving that I had come across when I was at college. These expressed a very simple and clear idea of what I was trying to say. It was clear because it was both a mental concept and a physical one. You can visualize spinning, weaving and cutting, and they can then be more readily turned into the abstract. These images can then be applied to the Goddesses of old to help explain their myths and legends. These ideas have now moved into my work with alchemy as a further refinement. While writing the book I have been continuing with this work, so many of the ideas expressed are part of an ongoing process that is constantly changing and evolving.

I have now ended up with a map that looks something like this. The Spinner spins the thread and is the creator. The Weaver forms the thread and makes the cloth. (The Spinner is the maker and the Weaver the shaper.) The Cutter is the finisher of the processes. It is then time to rest with the fruits of our being. We can then either move through the eye of the needle and go to the next level, which is that of the moon and the Queen of Alchemy, or we can repeat the weaving process again. To go through the doorway or across the abyss we have to meet with the Guardian of the Mysteries of Initiatrix, who carries us on to the next circuit of the spiral. As I said in the chapter on the God, very often it is a man or an emotional upset which in the wake of the feeling transports us. It can also be a strong vision of the Goddess, a dream, or a sudden change of circumstance. Once through this door, we meet the cycle of the Goddess again.

THE FOUR ALCHEMICAL QUEENS

The Virgin of Lights or the White Queen

She is the leader along the path who we follow to find our way in the darkness. She lights only every third light on the path, because we need to travel this path several times in order to find all that it has to offer. If we go from one light to the next, we miss the process of the journey and see only the lights, not the process and the cycle of the completion. We need to be travelling and feeling the cycle at the same time or we get bogged down with each of the symbols. The trees that she lights are the apple trees of the garden of Paradise or the garden of the Goddess Venus, and the lights are like the stars. If we study astrology, we find that not all the stars of the planets are relevant at the same time as they circle about our chart; they each have a time when they come into focus. The Virgin of Lights shows us how we can use this light to follow her path — the path of initiation — and how it does not need to be fully illuminated for us to see by. We do not need to know everything to be able to follow the path of initiation; the missing parts can be filled in later.

The Virgin of Lights is the embodiment of power and justice like the Tarot card Justice. She is also divine love, the love of humanity, which is the true force behind justice and power. She is the mistress of the garden. She chooses who is worthy and who is not. It is her lion or dragon that has to be fought.

The Black Queen and the Black Duchess

Here we meet the woman who helps and advises us so that we can change further. This is the Black Queen or Duchess, who helps us through the plays of death and resurrection. These go to the core of our being. It is very difficult as here we have to work with some of the most negative of the feminine deities. Society has projected on these figures all that it does not like or understand in the world.

She is the dark figure of the alchemical process, associated with dying and how this relates to our lives. These characters in novels and stories are associated with the idea of the infertile woman being a spinster, who becomes associated with death because she herself has not brought forth life. This can be a very sad place for women. They find that what is projected onto them by society is very negative, and this can at times be very difficult to get over in order to show the positive side of their nature. Many choose not to have children so that they can look after others, some so that they can devote all their energy to their work. This may be magic and the mysteries.

The Black Duchess of the alchemical tradition symbolizes all this, and she is the worker of wonders for the other to see.

I see the Black Duchess as like the Cutting Woman, and in meditation I have seen her with a sword. She is also like the Lady of the Lake or Morgan Le Fay — two of my favourite women. These women have swords which are a symbol that women can work well with. Below is a meditation to understand its positive aspects of justice and love.

Meditation of the Lady of the Sword

You are walking down a path through the forest. It is night and the trees are silhouetted against the moonlight. In the distance is a chapel that you are walking towards. It is devoted to the Goddess of the Forest and you go in and make a devotion to the Goddess in your own way. You ask that you may be able to meet the Lady of the Sword. The Goddess grants this request and tells you to make your way into the crypt of the chapel. Once there you make an invocation for her to appear. Before you the floor begins to dissolve, and you see a woman lying as if asleep; along the length of her torso is a sword. As you watch, the sword begins to glow. It appears that the sword connects the base chakra to the crown chakra, and the mind to the body.

As you continue to watch, the woman begins to wake and rise. When standing fully, she speaks to you and says that you can have the sword to cut through the mists of your life so that you can see the path more clearly. When you take the sword from her hands, you feel all your chakras starting to spin and then come into line and spin together. You also feel your body coming into line, and a feeling of deep peace begins to descend over you as the connection is made. You meditate on what you have received and then thanks are given to the Goddess and the Guardian. You make your way back to the present.

The Red Queen

She is the Queen of the menstrual mysteries, the woman with the power of life. She is also the Rose Queen and the Guardian of the Rose Garden. The rose garden is a symbol of the way that nature and women can work together. She is the balance of the elements so that creation and growth can take place. Her mysteries are the mysteries of menstruation; the creation within the self of the egg of our creativity. She is the guardian of the womb. Her mysteries are discussed in the Chapter 5.

The Eye Queen

She is the peacock-colour queen with a dress covered with the eyes of the peacock. In Alchemy this is the last process before the gold is made. The *prima materia* has all the colours of the rainbow.

In the Kalevala it is the Weaving Goddess who sits on the rainbow. Her weaving is described as:

> It is like the weaving of the moon spirit,
> the spinning of the sun spirit,
> the skill of the spirit of the great bear,
> and the finished work of the star spirit.[6]

In Greek mythology she is described as Iris the Goddess of the Rainbow:

Like fiery clouds, that flash with ruddy glare
Or Iris gliding through the purple air;
When loosely girt her dazzling mantle flows,
And against the sun in arching colours
glows.[7]

She is also the iris of the eye and the female soul, which is the organ of sight of both the visible and the invisible world. In Alchemy she is the female mercury and the bringer of death. She is associated with the rainbow path that the soul takes at death. She is both the beginning and the end of the Goddess spiral. It is she who helps us see behind the veil of the Goddess. It is her rainbow path that guides us behind this veil.

THE LIFTING OF THE VEIL

Many of the images we have of the Goddess are of veiled women. These veils mean that the woman is a sacred character whom we cannot look on directly, or who is withdrawn in some way. The wearing of the veil is now mainly associated with Islam, but was once part of the Goddess religion and her mysteries.

In the chymical wedding, Christian Rosenkreutz lifts the veil of the Goddess and becomes the next door-keeper of the mysteries. He has seen the conscious creative principle behind the manifestations of the natural world.[8] Once you have seen this, there is no going back. You can only serve the Goddess or the higher self, which works in conjunction with nature and the unfolding of life. To go through the veil is to become part of the mysteries and to accept your part in the scheme of things. It means that you become one with nature.

In the spring the veil of nature is lifted, and life starts to grow again. It is like the veil of Brigit's frost, or the snows of winter that melt away to reveal the earth again as it starts to grow into its beauty for the cycle to start again. The veil is like the web that connects everything together and makes the cycle of the seasons. The web of the leaf mirrors the underlying structure of the leaf of the universe. Leaves are like the veil of the tree, as flowers are the veil of the earth, and the stars the veil of the heavens. These veils cover the earth and hide her beauty and her darkness.

It is through these veils that we must pass to find the true wisdom of what the Goddess has to offer; this is the hidden mystery of the Goddess. The earth brings and sustains life, and is the *prima materia* of all being. It is dark yet it brings forth the light of the flowers and the leaves of growth. It is like when we walk into her forests, we go into the darkness and then find a grove of trees where the light can enter.

It is the same mystery again that is repeated over and over throughout the scheme of things. It is repeated in the rituals of the mysteries. The mysteries of going through the veil recreate the cycles of nature, showing as the sacredness of the original material and how we are a part of this process. It is from this darkness that the gold is obtained; by connecting with this darkness we can find our own inner gold with which we can try to heal ourselves from our anxieties. Through this healing process we can grow and change. It is the struggle that we as a new race on earth have to go through so that we can evolve.

These are the mysteries of the next level of the Goddess, of the realms of the stars, and of the Alchemical Queens. These are the mysteries that we have to work with to save the human race from destruction. This destruction is part of the mysteries of the Black Queen and alchemical putrefaction. I feel that it is time that we moved to the mysteries of the Red Queen and alchemical distillation. We should keep only the best from the past, and move on to a future where we are one world.

THE SILENT MYSTERIES

Here we have the inner vision of the Goddess, the visions that we get when we work with her mysteries. These come to us from the silence of the work of inner vision, but they are not silent in our mind and can be mixed with the Goddess actually talking to us. Sometimes she gives us a song of healing, sometimes a dance of creation.

Accessing this sort of material is up to the individual, and we all have our own ways of working. Finding the best way to work is a process of trial and error. I find that for particular moods certain techniques are best. My favourite is the use of sound, either a drum or chanting. I use this to start and then continue my journey in silence. Recently I have been introduced to the drumming tapes of Michael Harner,[1] which I find are very useful. The Foundation also produces a tape of women singing, which is a beautiful way of working. I use a technique whereby as the sound starts I allow myself to float down a tunnel and then find myself in another landscape. The tunnels and the way of entering them differ according to the mood, the purpose of the journey, and to the physical position that I am in when I take the journey.

In the literature of working with the mysteries, different cultures take different positions. In shamanic traditions of the past they lay down flat on their backs, whereas the Egyptians and the Western Mystery Tradition use the seated position. Some cultures use the crossed-leg position, and others the standing and the dancing positions. For further ideas on this a study of ancient sculptures in a museum is very worthwhile, as certain positions occur around the world for the Priestesses of the past. Lying down gives a sense of the earth and the energies that are held within. The sitting position gives information and knowledge, while standing can let you give the oracles of the Goddess.

In my contribution to *Voices from the Circle*[2] I have some ideas of how different landscapes are related to the different directions, which is an extension of this idea.

An article in the *Shaman's Drum*[3] described how if people sat in the same position they would have the same sort of vision. This is similar to the work that I have been experimenting with, but I was trying to find out which were the best positions for making contact with the Goddess.

Why do we see so many sculptures of the Goddess with her arms upraised looking like the womb within our bodies? Is this one of the old sacred positions of the Goddess? I believe it is because of the kind of contact that I have made with the Goddess when I have stood in this position.

The other position that I find fascinating is kneeling. Today this is associated with the Christian tradition, but is probably much older. I was reintroduced to this position at an art class run by Ruth Eisenhart, who saw it as the position of the twilight. When drawing a model in this position I was surprised by the different perspective I saw the world from. I then introduced it into my series of positions to work with when contacting the Goddess. It is a position of giving and of giving oneself to a higher power.

From these positions I have built up a repertoire of ways of working with the Goddess to give me different types of vision. This is a continuation of work that I started to find ways of contacting all the aspects of the Goddess. In this book I have used the aspects of the Spinner, the Weaver, the Cutter and the Silent One. At that time I was working with the more commonly used aspects of the Maiden, Mother and Crone. I started by trying to find out what these aspects meant to me and how they manifested in my life, beginning with the idea that all are one and the same. This means that what happens in one life is the same as in one year, one month or one day. For me this meant that I would go through the phases of the Maiden, Mother and Crone consecutively as my life progressed, but also that within one day I would go through all these phases. I then wanted to see how these worked within a daily, monthly and annual cycle.

It was easiest to see how these phases worked within the year as this is a long enough time to be aware of what was happening. I immediately realized that autumn is a time of great change for me. For example, it was on the last day of August that I gave up my job after eight years. Summer is a time for completing projects so that the new can start in the autumn. Spring is a time of resting, and I don't do much at this time. I often go on holiday, usually in February. Winter is a time when I go out and do courses, and am generally very sociable. It has given me the sense that I am very much at home in the dark, and that this is the time when I am at my most energetic. As a result of this realization I began to feel that I had a closer affiliation with the dark Goddess than the solar light Goddess. I confirmed this by looking at the things that I was interested in, like astrology, which can be seen as the study of the lights in the dark. Magic is often done in the dark, because one sees things differently at this time. I was also very attracted to the myths of the dark Goddesses.

At this point I would like to talk about the differences between the dark and the light. In many religions darkness has connotations of evil, and so things that are associated with the dark are also seen as evil. This is not true, but is often the way that one religion has taken over from another. The things that are sacred from the previous religion are put in the realm of taboo so that the new can take over. This is what has been done to religions based on the feminine. Nearly all the Goddesses of old now reside in some dark realm where they are said to be the forces of chaos. Chaos originally meant the great formless void or great deep of primordial matter. It is up to us all now to retrieve these mysteries that have been lost. The few exceptions that have managed to escape this fate have been the mothers of the Gods, who often seem unreal and unattainable in their saintliness, especially the Virgin Mary.

It is very important not to confuse darkness with evil, as the two are not the same. To me evil is the use of the sacred energies to hurt someone, to bring harm rather than healing. It is not the energy itself that is evil but the way that it is used. Often the evil is done unconsciously. I have certainly never met a consciously evil person.

It is very unfortunate that religions have often considered women evil or inferior to men. In Buddhism women are considered to be a lower order of incarnation, and in Christianity women have often been seen as the personification of evil.

E. Strachan in *The Freeing of the Feminine*[3, 4] says that we have to release the feminine from this dark prison. Von Franz states in *The Golden Ass*[5] that 'In the development of the Catholic Church the Virgin Mary is first an ordinary feminine being who slowly, through the historical process, is elevated to nearly divine rank. Thus, in the incarnation of the male God there is a descent into man, and in the incarnation of the female goddess, an ascent of an ordinary human being to a nearly divine realm.' Somehow through his descent the God has squashed the feminine underneath, and we are now struggling to get out from under his feet so we can ascend to the divine realms. We have to remember this at all times, otherwise we will be faced with taunts of being evil for following the religion of the Goddess, which is often associated with the worship of the Devil. Here we must each form our own answer to this accusation, as it will be made to us many times.

My answer is that I worship the Goddess as others worship the God. I see the divine as feminine rather than masculine, and the view that this is evil is propaganda put out by other religions about the nature-based pagan religions. I also go on to say that the Devil is part of the Christian Church only, and in some pagan religions there is a God on whose appearance the depiction of the Devil is based. This is the God of the forest, and many of the animals that used to live in the forests had horns; he is the God of these horned animals.

When I first started getting interested in the Goddess, I found it very difficult to decide what to say to others about my new religion. At the beginning of the 1980s it was less acceptable to be part of a religious group. The idea of Gaia had not taken off, and people at that time were not so concerned with their spiritual well-being. However, much has changed in the last ten years. I feel that the acceptance of the Goddess is largely due to feminists looking for positive images of women as role models.

It is in love that we can see the mysteries joining and hear the voice of the feminine. Love is the great force that guides us all. In the Renaissance it was expressed through the courtly romances and the Grail legends, later in the artists of the Romantic movement. Love was also present in the ascent of the Virgin Mary and other female saints. Here we find the black madonna who was the original version of this figure and shrines to her can be found throughout the world. In recent times there have been visions of the Virgin by people other than priests and priestesses. These have been recorded regularly throughout the world in such diverse places as Yugoslavia and China, as well as in predominantly Catholic countries. At times, though, the manifestations of which women have seen or heard have landed them in mental asylums — another way of oppressing women's individuality and love.

This chapter is called 'the mysteries of silence' because so much of our knowledge of the Goddess has been silenced. We now have to find her voice and her vision again to create a balance in society. When we have a culture that accepts the Goddess it will enable us to question the values and change the structure of society.

In earlier cultures there have often been artistic representations of deity. This has been an important part of religion. I feel that it is very important to be able to visualize the diety with which you are working, as this makes her appear more solid. This can be done either with the use of images of the Goddess or with symbols that represent her. This is where altars to the Goddess are so helpful: we can set up within our home a place where the Goddess can live. An altar is also symbolically a sacred place within ourselves, which can provide us with the faith, experience and knowledge that we need for our lives to feel complete.

With faith, the Goddess will come, and we will then have the experience with which to continue the work. She will give us the visions that will guide our further study and lead to knowledge. For me working alone would have been very difficult, and I owe a great debt to those that I have worked with in groups who have given me the support to continue the work. Groups, however, are not easy to work in and require a strong commitment. They are plagued with all sorts of problems and require a great deal of tolerance, mainly because everyone sees the deity differently and an individual's discussion of this personal experience is very difficult to understand by another who has not had the same experience. These differences can turn into personal antagonisms that can be devastating.

However, I do suggest that people become part of a group, as this is a very intense way of working with the Goddess. Finding a group is more difficult, but there is a list of contacts in the appendix.

WORKING WITH THE GODDESS

A very good place to start work is your own name. Find out if there is a Goddess whom you were named after, or commemorated on the day of your birth, or associated with the area where you live. My name is derived from the Latin *Felicitas*, which is an aspect of Venus. I have always been interested in the Goddess of the Earth, and see Venus as one of these aspects. My birthday is during the period of the Mania, a Roman festival to the dead, which gives some hints as to why I find other worlds so fascinating. I live in an area of London that is associated with the Horned God and Goddess, which provides a nature contact. (For details of dates see, *The Year of the Goddess* by Lawrence Durdin-Robertson.[6] Your local library will have information on local history.)

From this beginning one can begin to find one's dominant interest in the Goddess. Mine is very much through contact with the earth, in the caves and the dark places of the earth, and with the other worlds that exist there. These were the things that I responded to most strongly in reading books on the Goddess and which came up most often in my journeys and dreams. My love of the dark is continued in my love of the stars, part of another world. Through this, I came into contact with Astraea, the Goddess of Justice and Love.

WORKING WITH ENERGY

Magical energy is a very profound and difficult thing to describe in words, as we all perceive it in different ways. Firstly it is perceived through our primary sense; for some people this is vision, for others hearing, for others touch, and for a few taste or smell. Time is well spent deciding which is your primary sense and working with it in different situations. Learning to feel energy is the first step in the journey of learning how to work with and perceive energy for magical use and healing.

Energy is most easily felt in a group setting, where it is stronger because of the numbers involved and where you can get instant feedback as to what happened and whether your experiences were similar to others in the group. This is better than totally relying on yourself at first, although if you feel the true energy you will know immediately as it can be very strong.

Energies can often be seen when working in groups as moving around the circle when the work is in progress. When energy is being raised for healing it is at its strongest and most visible. It looks like a spinning mass moving round and round the room, usually white light; when reaching its zenith it becomes cone-shaped and moves even faster.

Once this sort of energy has begun to be raised it can be worked with. This is where the spinning, weaving and cutting comes in. What I have described so far in these experiences is the spinning process of getting the energy started. The weaving process is longer and more complex as it is based on assumptions that the energy is there and that it can be altered. In healing, for instance, the energy needs to be woven so that it can be concentrated on a particular part of the body that needs to be healed. This is done by the healer, and the energy that is circulated is woven together like strands of thread so that it is stronger. So from wildly floating around the room it starts to flow in a contained spinning circle, like a spiralling thread. The energy is then concentrated by the mind and directed into the part of the body that needs to be healed. Energy left over can be stored in the body of the person receiving the healing like skeins of wool, so that when needed it can be called upon.

BEING A PRIESTESS OF THE GODDESS

I don't think that I know when I first became a Priestess; it felt like a growing process. In a sense I always knew that I was a Priestess and that this was what I was going to be. I had an inner feeling as soon as I found the mysteries that I was going to follow the path of the Goddess and the women's mysteries. I made this decision early on and it has never changed. In everything that I do now I look for the Goddess's presence in that situation; she is always there in one form or another. So in every situation that I find myself in, I can perform my priestly functions.

What are Priestessly functions?

- Seeing the sacred and the divine in all things and especially in all people
- Helping others to find the sacred in themselves
- Mediating the divine
- Worshipping the divine in all things
- Being the divine
- Being the friend of the divine
- Being the voice of the divine
- Expressing the divine in ways that others can understand
- Living according to one's own moral code
- Allowing others to live as they like
- Healing ourselves so that we can heal the earth

What is the divine?

I believe in a divine power that exists in the universe and that is the primary creative force. For me this force is feminine and is part of all beings in the universe. It is this force that shapes and creates the universe. It is not a power in the usual sense of the word but a receptive principle that is continuously there yet ever-changing. It does not create form but allows space for individual things to shape and make themselves. It provides the energy for these things to happen. The Goddess and her archetype are expressions of this force.

WORKING WITH THE GODDESS WHEN WE ARE DEPRESSED

By looking for and finding the strength of the Goddess we can raise our spirits. This can be done in a variety of ways; the main problem is to get ourselves sufficiently motivated to start the whole process. I have found that supportive friends can often trigger the start of this process. Periods of depression are often a sign of change which can be frightening, but once the process has started it becomes much easier.

How to get the process started

Sometimes we have to realize that we cannot do the process alone, although in a sense we are also alone when we are working with others. Sometimes we just have to take a deep breath and jump. One mistake that I have frequently made is to think that by making or allowing one change, everything will be very different afterwards. I know now that the changes are very subtle at first and then gain momentum as we feel their positivity. Working with the changing faces of the Goddess can help this process. As we change we move with her faces, and we can work towards finding her more positive aspects.

When in the throes of darkness and despair, we can try to move ourselves into the colours of the Rainbow Goddess. This at first requires much faith that things will get better, that we have not lost everything and that we can find the positive again.

I worked with the Weaving Goddess Orchil when I was very down and thought the world was against me. In a meditation I found myself curled up under her loom. When I looked up I saw her weaving away at the rainbows of dreams, and how she kept going even though humanity insisted on making their rainbows very dirty. I saw how easy it was to clean my rainbow and that I too could hope for what I wanted. I then saw that her loom was like a great protection around my house and myself and that I could use this to protect myself from the influences that I didn't want entering my life. She then wove a cocoon around me to make me feel secure with the work that I was doing and the truth of the visions that I was having.

Sometimes depression is caused by the process of cutting ourselves off from something or someone so that we can allow the process of change to happen. This is the resting stage before we start on a new cycle. I often put off the final cut as I am frightened that the changes that this cutting brings will not be as positive as I would like. I have at these times lost trust in my own beliefs. At the time of cutting I often feel more like the warrior than the wise woman. When I start cutting I am prepared to sacrifice all, allowing nothing to get in the way of the task that I want to complete. This is a very frightening feeling as I know the results could be destructive as well as constructive.

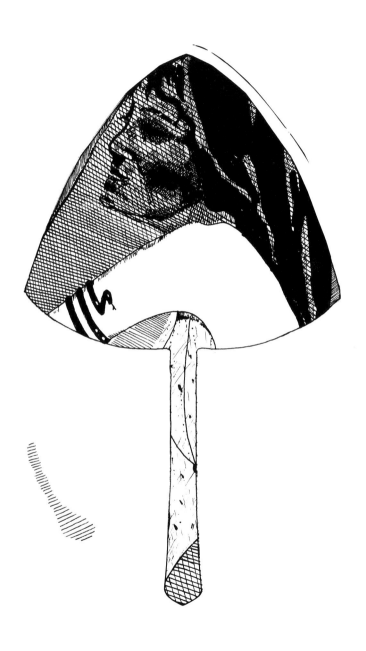

9

THE ABYSS

Going over the abyss symbolizes change in our lives, including physical death. Death is another taboo subject like menstruation. We rarely think or talk of our death, yet our ideas about death can influence the way that we live our lives.

In the cycle that I have outlined for the Weaving Goddess I have written about the ending of the cycle and the resting before going onto the next stage. In the usual way of things this is not an actual death, but sometimes it can be. This is the time when one chooses to go to another realm or plane for the next phase of the cycle. As no one knows what happens after death all our ideas about it are very subjective.

My experience of death is very limited, but when I was with a friend who was dying, I felt the soul or the life force leaving his body. After this the body itself died as a separate event. In some religions these two events are given separate rites. I thought that it was important to give the soul permission to leave, and then with friends to give the body a ceremony that befitted its time alive.

In some magical thought the time of death is a celebration that the soul has came to an end of its cycle on earth. I did feel with one friend that their dying came when they had finished the healing work that they had to do on the planet. This did make their death easier to understand than the death of another friend, where I do not understand why she died so young.

Being with someone who was so close to dying was a very profound experience for me. The energy and the emotions around the person were so strong that I felt I hardly knew what was happening. I had thought that these would become weaker and weaker as the person neared dying, but I found that the reverse was true and they actually increased. It was as though someone from the place that he was going to came and collected him. My inner being saw this as a golden light, which surrounded the soul and took it to another place. This was one of the strongest mystical experiences that I have ever had. I did not feel sad or upset at the time, because it confirmed an inner feeling that there was something after death. I also felt that he had gone to a place where there was a great deal of happiness. The main result was a personal confirmation of the idea that there is a separate spirit in the body, that the two separate at death, and that the spirit does go on to another place. I also felt that it is very important to have a proper ceremony for the deceased. All things that end should have a proper ceremony to mark their ending.

WOMEN WITH WINGS AND SWORDS

The angel, the woman with the wings, the woman with the sword, the woman with the cauldron, and the woman with the crystal ball — these are the women that we have the potential to become. They are the future, they are ourselves: the wild, free women that are within us.

The goal is to become free, to release ourselves from the prison of society. We can then fly to the stars, go and live in a cave or in the forest, and make our potions. Then we become the woman that we truly are inside, and are able to fulfil our own destiny and enable others to find theirs. This is our service to the earth and the spirit of creation. That is the divine Creatrix of the universe. She is the one that creates but it is up to us what we do with that creation. It is our destiny and our choice whether we fulfil it or not. She is the one that finishes the contract but we can negotiate with her when this time should be. Some do this as a conscious process others unconsciously.

This is a good time to contact the ancestors and to heal the problems of the family and the past — the problems that have been caused by humanity which have meant that the human race is now a parasite on the planet.

Nature created us for a reason and I would like to find out what this was for. There are all these different worlds that we live in and we all live in them separately. We have to be able to all live in them together with no separation and no barriers to travelling from one to another. They are all equal. We are all equal. This is what we will find if we work together and work with our community. It can be achieved if we try. We need to work from

Figure 10 *Spindle works*

the grass roots or the individual to the collective. This is the way of the future; it is the way of finding what we want individually both for our lives and for the magic. We need to continue so that this magic can be part of the way that we live our lives. Magic is the energy and process of transformation. For a long while it was thought that the process was the same for men and women, but Jungians believe it is similar yet different for both. A man can free the woman but the woman must also free herself from the unconscious. A woman is attached to the mother and feminine society, and must free herself if she is to develop. The man must also free himself from the mother if he is to find his own masculinity. A woman must find her identification with the father and then free herself from this, as does a man. Both must find themselves at the centres of their being, and start the individuation process again if it is to be of lasting value.

We can see this process in the myth of the Fates, who are

represented by the Spinner, the Weaver and the Cutter. These also represent the first three phases of the moon; the hidden/resting aspect is the fourth.

THE SPINNER

The Spinner is identified with the feminine; to sit and spin is a very maternal activity. To sort the thread is to relate and join things together. The woman tends and cares for the thread; she provides the space in which it can grow and form the cauldron of creation, her body. She gives it the security of formation and the container in which it can explore. The spinner finds that this relationship gives her the fulfilment she needs. Once this relationship to the thread of life is made conscious, the woman can use this to lead her to the next stage of the process. We have to spin enough thread to make the ball of wool, and then we have to unwind it and dye it to start the weaving process.

We then see the fruits of our labour and are ready to show the process to others and show them how they too can continue with the spinning. We then have to cut the wool and unwind the ball so that we can dye it and wash it ready for weaving. This is the time of rest before the next stage when we go through the abyss for the next turn around the cycle.

THE WEAVER

The process of weaving helps to make us independent in that we have to set up our own looms. We have to thread our own warp threads onto which we can weave our own weft threads. We start to make our own patterns in life, which are then acknowledged by others. This is a process that we do alone, although we also make friends and relate to others in the weaving process. We stop worrying about our relationships with others as we peruse the patterns and our understanding of them in our lives. We can see the ups and downs of our lives in relation to our thoughts. We can see our own creativity growing before us, which is part of ourself yet separate.

Spinning in the weaving we are unwinding the threads so that the weaving can take place, forming the threads for the shuttle so the process can continue. Cutting in the weaving we have to cut the threads of the warp and the weft; to shape the tapestry we also have to cut out the mistakes that we make.

166

THE CUTTER

The fabric is woven and all is now contained within it. There is now a relationship to the work which is more than the making, and it has a magic of its own. The weaving in the cutting is the change of colour or the change of the pattern; stopping one pattern and changing to another within the same design without losing sight of the finished product.

ALCHEMICAL QUEENS

When we have finished we have to wait between the worlds, in the middle or in neutral. We are immersed in the environment that we have created and the spirit that has come from our creation. We are tired after the act of creation and take a rest. We are swept on by the energy we have produced to the next phase of the journey. We go into a state of turmoil as we fight to be the person that we want to be, but we need peace so that we can understand what is happening. We can now contact the forces of nature again in their pure form. We flow with the energies of the life that we are living. We can see beyond the veil and look upon creation with fresh eyes.

This is the individuation process in the symbolism of the Weaving Goddess. To make this process work within and outside ourselves we need to weave together all the energies, to create the true self. We need to work with all the levels, both inner and outer, so we can live our true self at all times. It is the weaving together of the three levels into our lives that is important, so that we can heal ourselves and help others heal themselves.

To contact the true energy of the Goddess and her wisdom we have to be in the place of true self. It is from this place that we can become the voice of the Goddess, and she can speak to us all.

> The Goddess speaks to us in many
>   ways.
> We can hear her talking to us
> in the rustling of the leaves in the
>   wind.
> Is it the wind or is it the tree that is
>   talking to us?
> At times she calls us to her council
>   to hear her sacred words.

167

She calls us to her meeting places so
we may hear her voice.
Now it has become the voice of pain,
*   as so few hear the call.*
Why can we no longer hear her call?
How have we become so cut off?
Listen to her crying, crying for the
*   love that she once knew.*
Let us follow the call and see where
*   it will lead us to,*
so that we may learn to be free.
Just go.
We can leave the washing.
We can leave the work.
Let's go, let's follow the sacred call
— go to the places that it leads us to.
Let's follow, let us find the part that
*   is missing.*
We walk along the road,
we follow the overgrown pathways,
we walk to the sacred grove of the
*   goddess.*
When we arrive we find that it is
*   overgrown,*
no one has been to visit for years.
We clear the centre so that we can
*   find a space on which to rest.*
Here we are at the place that the call
*   has brought us to.*
We sit,
we rest,
we wait
and we wait.
We wait to meet with the person that
*   has called us here,*
Where are they?
Why are they not here to greet us?
What is wrong?
Are we at the wrong place?
We hear the call again,
we follow and arrive at a cave.
A woman is inside,
she calls again,
we walk forward.

168

She sees us
and thanks us for coming to her call,
but she cannot leave;
the time is not right.
we must sit and wait,
wait and sit.
She tells us her story.
It is the story of your life.
She is the mirror.
It is the mirror of you as the
*   Goddess.*
You year her voice telling you to
release yourself and become her.
Live now, not later.
Don't hide in the cave any longer,
come out,
release me.
Accept the challenge of life,
the challenge to find and leave,
to move on,
to die and be reborn.

REFERENCES

This booklist contains some of the books that I have read during my research. It also contains contact addresses of specialist groups.

Introduction

1. *The Spiral Dance*, Starhawk (Harper & Row, 1979)
2. Matriarchy Research and Reclaim Network Newsletter c/o Blanche, Cloverley House, Erwood, Powys LD2 3EZ, Wales
3. *Arcadia*, C. Layland (Daniel and Co., 1929)

Other books of interest

The Holy Book of Women's Mysteries, Z. Budapest (Hale, 1990)
Elements of the Goddess, C. Matthews (Element, 1989)
The Cosmic Mother, M.Sjöo and B. Moor (Harper & Row, 1975)

Chapter 1

1. *The Mystic Spiral*, J. Purce (Thames & Hudson, 1974)
2. *Alchemy* S. Klossowski de Roller (Thames & Hudson, 1989)
3. *The Goddess*, C. Downing (Crossroad, 1984)
4. *First Steps in Ritual* D. Ashcroft-Nowicki (The Aquarian Press, 1990, 2nd edn)
5. *Isis in the Greco-Roman World*, R. Witt (Thames & Hudson, 1971)
6. *The Greek Myths*, R. Graves (Penguin, 1983)
7. *The Silver Bough*, F. McNeill (Maclellan, 1977, vol.2, p.57)
8. *Keltic Folk and Faerie Tales*, K. Naddair (Century, 1987)

9. *Women's Dictionary of Symbols*, B. Walker (Harper & Row, 1988)
10. *The Gods of the Egyptians*, W. Budge (Dover, 1969)
11. *The Language of the Goddess*, M. Gimbutas (Thames & Hudson, 1989)
12. Ibid, p.221

Chapter 2

1. *The Golden Ass*, Apuleius (Penguin, 1969)
2. *The Hero of a Thousand Faces*, Joseph Campbell, (Abacus, 1975)
3. *The Language of the Goddess*, M. Gimbutas (Thames & Hudson, 1989)

The House of Net runs a Priestess correspondence training course. For details write to BCM, Box 6812, London WC1N 3XX.

Chapter 3

1. *A Dictionary of Symbols*, J.E. Cirlot (Routledge, 1981)

Chapter 4

1. Tapestry in the Victoria and Albert Museum, London
2. *Maps to Ecstasy*, G. Roth (The Aquarian Press, 1990)
3. *A Dictionary of Symbols*, J. Cirlot (Routledge, 1981)
4. *Python: A Study of Delphic Myth and its Origins*, J. Fontenrose (University of California Press, 1980)
5. *The Language of the Goddess*, M. Gimbutas (Thames & Hudson, 1989)
6. *Aromatherapy: An A–Z*, P. Davis (Daniel & Co., 1988, p.167)
7. *Poems and Dramas*, F. Macleod (Heinemann, 1929)
8. *Woman and Nature: The Roaring Inside Her*, S. Griffin (Women's Press, 1984)
9. *Thinking Like a Mountain: Towards a Council of All Beings*, J. Seed et al (Heretic Books, 1988)
10. *The Politics of Inner Experience*, J.F. Phipps (Green Print, 1990)

Other books of interest

Snakefat and Knotted Threads, K. Koppana (Mandragora Dimensions, Finland)
Traditional Scottish Dyes, J. Frazer (Canongate, 1985)
Keltic Folk and Faerie Tales K. Naddair, (Century, 1987)

Groups

Women's Environmental Network, 287 City Road, London EC1V 1LA
London Ecology Centre, 45 Shelton Street, London WC2H 9HJ

Chapter 5

1. *The Wise Wound*, P. Shuttle and P. Redgrove (Gollancz, 1978)
2. *Menstrual Taboo*, Asphodel (The Matriarchy Study Group, out of print)
3. *The Moonspinners*, M. Stewart (Coronet, 1962)
4. *First Steps in Ritual*, D. Ashcroft-Nowicki (The Aquarian Press, 1990, 7th edn)
5. *The Poisoned Womb*, J. Elkington (Viking, 1984)
6. *The Female Eunuch*, G. Greer (Paladin, 1971)
7. *The Wise Wound*, p.178
8. *Patterns in Natural Family Planning*, B. Annese and H. Danzer (Patterns Publishing (CA. USA))

Other publications of interest

Snakepower Magazine, 5856 College Ave., 138 Oakland CA, 94618, USA
Woman of Power Magazine, PO Box 827, Cambridge, MA 02238, USA

Chapter 6

1. *The Psychological Stages of Feminine Development*, E. Neumann Analytical Psychology Club N.Y., 1954, pp.63–97
2. Ibid., p.74
3. *The Feminine* A. Ulanov (Northwestern 1971)
4. Ibid., p.276
5. *The Wise Wound*, P. Shuttle and P. Redgrove (Gollancz, 1978)

Chapter 7

1. *The Classics of Western Spirituality*, Hadewijch (SPCK, 1980, p.286)
2. *Gold in the Crucible*, D. Green (Element, 1989)
3. Hadewijch
4. *The Elements of the Goddess*, C. Matthews (Element, 1989)
5. *Circle of Nine*, C. Gilchrist (Dryad, 1988)
6. *Kalevala*, Poem 24 (OUP, 1989)
7. *The Myths of Greece and Rome*, H. Guerber (Harrap & Co., 1908)
8. *The Rose Cross and the Goddess*, G. Knight (The Aquarian Press, 1985)

Other publications of interest

The Hermetic Journal, PO Box 375, Headington, Oxford OX3 5PW

Chapter 8

1. The Foundation for Shamanic Studies, Box 670, Beldon Station, Norwalk, Connecticut 06852, USA
2. *Voices from the Circle*, C. Matthews and P. Jones (eds.), (Aquarian, 1990)
3. Trance States and Spirit Journeys, Felicitas D. Goodman, *Shaman's Drum*, Spring 1990.
4. *Freeing the Feminine*, E. Strachan (Lambarum, 1985).
5. *The Golden Ass*, Apuleins (Penguin, 1990).
6. Lawrence Durdin-Roberts, *The Year of the Goddess* (The Aquarian Press, 1990).

USEFUL ADDRESSES

Fellowship of Isis, Clonegal Castle, Enniscorthy, Co. Wexford, Eire

The Foundation for Shamanic Studies, Box 670, Belden Station, Norwalk, Connecticut 06852, USA

The House of Net, BCM, Box 6812, London WC1N 3XX

Matriarchy Research and Reclaim Network Newsletter, c/o Blanche, Cloverley House, Erwood, Powys LD2 3EZ, Wales

London Ecology Centre, 45 Shelton St, London WC2H 9HJ

Women's Environmental Network, 287 City Rd, London EC1V 1LA

Felicity Wombwell, 1 Ravenstone Rd, London N8 0JT *(please send SAE for reply)*